W9-BCL-101

RIVERS IN AMERICAN LIFE AND TIMES

The Colorado River

The Columbia River

The Hudson River

The Mississippi River

The Missouri River

The Ohio River

Mississippi River Basin

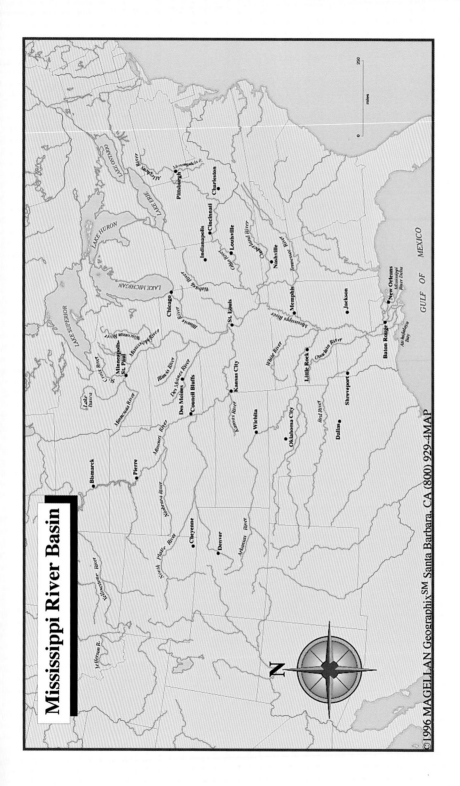

©1996 MAGELLAN GeographixSM Santa Barbara, CA (800) 929-4MAP

THE MISSISSIPPI RIVER

Tim McNeese

CHELSEA HOUSE
PUBLISHERS
A Haights Cross Communications Company
Philadelphia

FRONTIS: This late twentieth-century map of the Mississippi River basin shows the path of the river and its tributaries across the United States.

CHELSEA HOUSE PUBLISHERS

VP, NEW PRODUCT DEVELOPMENT Sally Cheney
DIRECTOR OF PRODUCTION Kim Shinners
CREATIVE MANAGER Takeshi Takahashi
MANUFACTURING MANAGER Diann Grasse

Staff for THE MISSISSIPPI RIVER

EXECUTIVE EDITOR Lee Marcott
PRODUCTION EDITOR Megan Emery
PHOTO EDITOR Sarah Bloom
SERIES DESIGNER Keith Trego
COVER DESIGNER Keith Trego
LAYOUT 21st Century Publishing and Communications, Inc.

A Haights Cross Communications ⟋ Company

www.chelseahouse.com

First Printing

9 8 7 6 5 4 3 2 1

Library of Congress Cataloging-in-Publication Data applied for.

ISBN 0-7910-7723-3 HC   0-7910-8004-8 PB

CONTENTS

1

The River's First Inhabitants

It lies at the heart of the North American continent. The Mississippi River is one of the greatest rivers in the world, a watershed covering more than 1.2 million square miles. River systems in 32 states and two Canadian provinces provide its immense flow. As one of America's most significant natural features, it is the third-longest river in the world and the greatest river in the Northern Hemisphere. Its waters originate from places as far apart as the Appalachian Mountains in the east to the commanding heights of the Rockies in the west. Dozens of tributary rivers, including such significant systems as the Missouri, Ohio, Tennessee, Cumberland, Illinois, Arkansas, and Red deliver their contents to the collective waters of the Mississippi. European explorers who paddled their canoes from other rivers into the great water road called the Mississippi a "gathering of waters." From its source at Lake Itasca, located in northern Minnesota, the Mississippi meanders along endless twists and turns in its watery course of approximately 2,340 miles until it reaches its southern mouth and drains its muddy contents into the Gulf of Mexico.

The Mississippi is an ecological wonder: It and its tributary rivers provide a banked refuge for hundreds of plants and animals found nowhere else in the world. From the air, millions of migratory birds, as well as waterfowl, follow the river's course and its lowland marshes and swamps as a supportive habitat. Experts estimate that 40 percent of North America's waterfowl, including ducks, geese, swans, and wading birds, use the Mississippi River as a corridor of migration. Its waters support more than 300 varieties of fish, including the unique species called paddlefish, found in no other river. Today, the balance of nature within and along the Mississippi faces constant challenge and threat for survival.

Just as this immense river has provided home and support for countless species of flora and fauna, it has also been the home of millions of people. Early Native Americans dotted the river's banks with their villages. Today, millions of people populate its great river cities, including Minneapolis–St. Paul, St. Louis,

Since it first started to flow, the Mississippi River has been home and a resource for countless plants, animals, and humans. By the nineteenth century, it was even a center of commerce, providing a route of trade and transportation for steamboats. As this painting from 1883 shows, farms, homes, and riverboat docks filled the river's lush banks.

Memphis, and New Orleans. In between, the river is home to hundreds of towns large and small, many torn from the pages of American history, including LaCrosse, Wisconsin; Dubuque and Davenport, Iowa; Hannibal, Missouri; Cairo, Illinois; and Vicksburg and Natchez, Mississippi. For thousands of years, humans have made their homes along and within sight of the banks of the Mississippi River. Indian tribes hunted and fished in its waters and established villages, including such significant towns as Cahokia, in Illinois, located in the area of modern-day St. Louis and home to as many as 20,000 people. Early European arrivals established trading forts, missionary centers, and village outposts. In the early nineteenth century, American steamboats reached its waters, creating an enduring image of steam-powered trade and transportation as great white boats sporting red-painted paddle wheels and black smokestacks plied up and down the Mississippi. The river became a golden highway of commerce for countless Americans. That same century witnessed the upheaval of the Civil War as the river became a winding ribbon of conflict and its towns were introduced to a new type of rivercraft: ironclad gunboats.

Within the past century, the Mississippi's commercial river traffic changed from steamboats to tows and its recreational craft reduced. It also experienced its most serious floods. Modern river experts have attempted to make its course permanent, tried to control its flow, and established great dikes along both its banks. The mighty Mississippi, however, has remained an uncontrollable river, one refusing to be tamed. It is a river that today faces serious challenges, both natural and man-made. For many, the Mississippi continues to provide inspiration and mystery. Writer and Mississippi traveler Tom Weil observes how each passing generation that has experienced the great American waterway witnessed a river unique to its time:

> The Mississippi presents a paradox of change and continuity. Never ceasing to change, the restless river from one day to the next revises itself, here crumbling a bank, there adding a bar, now swelling its currents and then once again resuming its slow rhythmic flow . . . So great have the changes in the Mississippi's channel been over just three centuries that much of the 1,300 miles floated in 1682 by LaSalle, the first European to travel down the river to its mouth, now lie on dry land. Ceaseless change, over thousands of years, gradually forged the Mississippi.[1]

Today, the Mississippi remains the ever-changing, organic wonder it has always been. This great interior waterway of American history is, in the words of the nineteenth-century historian Francis Parkman, a "dark and inexorable river . . . rolling like a destiny, through its realms of solitude and shade."[2]

Despite its magnificent scope and length, the Mississippi is a river like all other rivers in the world—it has a point of origin and an ending, the mouth of the river. Like many of the natural features found on maps of the United States today, the Mississippi did not always exist. Various forms of the river may have flowed across portions of the United States hundreds of thousands of years ago, but topographers and river experts estimate today's Mississippi River to be approximately 12,000 years old. It was formed largely during the most recent stage of the Great Ice Age, a glacial period called the Wisconsin Glaciation. That ice period began about 75,000 years ago and petered out around 10,000 B.C., when the climate of North America experienced a significant change. During this era of deep freeze, giant animals, such as hairy mammoths and woolly mastodons, roamed the region of modern-day Minnesota and Wisconsin. Some of the prehistoric fish living in this frozen region—including long-nosed and short-nosed gar, sturgeon, and paddlefish—can be found in the Mississippi River today.

During the last days of the Wisconsin Glaciation, the great glacier shelves began to melt. Many of these ancient glaciers were one to two miles thick and covered hundreds of thousands of square miles of territory. The water unleashed from the glacial melting left cold-water reservoirs in low places, creating great lakes and a vast inland sea called Lake Agassiz, which covered northwest Minnesota, portions of North Dakota, and the Canadian provinces of Manitoba, Saskatchewan, and Ontario, a region of more than 200,000 square miles. Waters from this immense postglacial lake formed the Glacial River Warren, which, in time, cut a trough that later formed the Minnesota River. The early Mississippi River would later flow into the valley created by the River Warren. As the glaciers continued to shrink, their melting waters created the extensive river system that drained into the Mississippi Valley basin.

In his book *Life on the River*, historian Norbury L. Wayman describes the natural processes that worked to create the Mississippi:

> Drift deposits, created during the runoff of these waters, made a scouring action, causing rolling prairies, and level plains resulted where shallow lakes and marshes had formerly existed. The plains that gradually rise from the Missouri River at the western boundary of Missouri, and which reach an elevation exceeding five thousand feet above sea level in the foothills of the Rocky Mountains, were washed very heavily, with much surface material being distributed to the central valley and filling the lower Mississippi basin. These surface deposits contained considerable loam and chemical material required for plant growth and resulted in the rich alluvial river-bottom lands along the western rivers.[3]

This prolonged process of water and mineral distribution created a shallower river basin. Experts estimate that the Mississippi River Valley was approximately 250 feet deeper than its modern-day counterpart. After hundreds of years, this tremendous waterflow of melting glaciers subsided, leaving behind the Mississippi River as the most significant river in the region.

Human beings began migrating into the Mississippi Valley during the time of the glacial meltdown. These early arrivals were hunting societies, nomadic peoples who tracked the big game of the period using stone-tipped spears. Evidence of these early occupants of the Mississippi Valley includes their projectile points as well as their skeletal remains. Little is known of these wandering prehistoric peoples beyond the rudimentary physical discoveries.

The oldest known occupants of the Mississippi River basin to remain in the region and establish a continuous history of settlement were those peoples archaeologists call the Mound Builders. About A.D. 700, a mound-building culture called the Mississippian Culture emerged. This era provides the historical link between the ancient peoples of the Mississippi Valley and

NAMING AMERICA'S GREATEST RIVER

The nineteenth-century American writer Mark Twain, author of the semi-autobiographical novel *Life on the Mississippi*, described the Mississippi River as a "wonderful book (with) a new story to tell every day." Just as the Mississippi has redefined itself through the centuries, tracing new channels and abandoning old courses, so it has experienced renaming as the people of each era christened it with new meaning.

It was the Native Americans who first named the great river the "Mississippi." The Ojibway Indians of northern Minnesota used the name "Messipi," which translated as "Big River." The name united two of their words—*Mech-e*, meaning "great" or "large," and *Se-be*, meaning "river." Some Indian linguists identify another source for the river's name, referring to the name "May-see-see-bee," which translates as "The Father of Running Waters."

Still other names have been used to identify the Mississippi. An early Spanish explorer, Alonzo Alvarez de Pineda, called the Mississippi the "Rio del Espiritu Santo"—the River of the Holy Spirit. When early French explorers reached the river, they gave it a religious name, "Rivière de St. Louis." By the late nineteenth century, many river people, especially southern blacks who lived along the Mississippi's lower course, were calling the lazy-flowing, mile-wide waterway "Old Man River."

Whatever the names given for the greatest of American rivers, they usual refer to the river with respect and admiration, paying homage to its size, its age, and vitality.

the modern tribal groups that have come down to the present time, such as the Choctaws, Chickasaws, Natchez, and others. The geographical center of this Mound Builder culture was in what are now the states of Mississippi and Tennessee, as well as Alabama.

This third era of Mound Builders set themselves apart from their predecessors by building a unique type of mound. They constructed earthen pyramids. Earlier Mound Builders also typically constructed their projects as burial sites, but the Mississippians erected their mounds as temples and as dwelling sites for their chiefs.

The Mississippians introduced new crops to the Mississippi Valley. They raised corn, which had been brought in from central Mexico, and with the arrival of this staple crop, the Native Americans of the region became serious agriculturists. Such crops allowed the Mississippian peoples to remain in permanent towns and villages, where their mounds took on special significance as places for the living rather than the dead.

One of the most important native cities of the Mound Builders was constructed near the site of modern-day St. Louis. This metropolis of ancient America was known as Cahokia. This native culture site

> was situated on the eastern bank of the Mississippi River . . . It covered six square miles and boasted an ancient population of approximately 25,000 people. Archaeologists have unearthed at least eighty-five mounds at this Mississippian site. Considering that this culture did not have a practical use of the wheel or animals to carry heavy loads, this building accomplishment is stupendous. The mounds were created by the labors of thousands of workers, who carried baskets of earth up the incline, depositing their load at the mound's ever-increasing summit. Over time, the city declined and was eventually abandoned. The reasons for its collapse as an ancient population center are not clear.[4]

The mounds erected at Cahokia towered over the local landscape. Perhaps numbering as many as 150, only about 85 mounds remain somewhat intact today. One of the Cahokia mounds stood as tall as a 10-story building. Typically, the Cahokia mounds were built with sloping sides and featured a flat top, where special temples were built, as well as public structures, homes for the local ruler, and sometimes even statues. Below these towering mounds, the Cahokia people lived in their own homes, ran their shops and schools, and walked along well-laid-out streets.

The central population was 25,000, and an equal number of inhabitants probably lived in the satellite communities scattered around the Cahokia site. Such an elaborate city–state complex was constructed along the banks of the Mississippi for obvious reasons. The Mississippi was the primary highway for travel and trade for this important civilization. Cahokian canoes could carry trade goods up- and downriver, making connections with other peoples over great distances and paddling their boats up the neighboring Missouri and Illinois Rivers. Experts explain that the people of Cahokia built their community near the Mississippi River for the same reasons that the modern-day city of St. Louis was later established by Europeans. As one Cahokia archaeologist has stated, "It stands above floodwaters and is surrounded by fertile bottomlands, yet it lies close to the junction of three rivers—the Mississippi, Missouri, and Illinois. . . . Wherever you find a modern city along the river system, you can bet Indians had a town there too."[5]

The Mississippian Mound Builder era reached its zenith during the 1500s. Several of the larger mound-based communities along the Mississippi Valley fell apart by that time, but others survived. Sites such as Cahokia were eventually abandoned as too complex to maintain. The people who lived in these former civilizations scattered and became more like their primitive neighbors, other tribes of Native Americans that still relied largely on hunting for survival. Many of these smaller tribal units survived until the arrival of the Europeans in the 1500s.

Most of the Mound Builders of the Mississippian Culture era died out by the sixteenth century, but one tribe did survive. Known as the Natchez, these Mound Builders were located down the Mississippi River near modern-day Natchez, Mississippi. The Natchez peoples numbered several thousand in the 1540s, when they were visited by the Spanish explorer Hernando de Soto. These Lower Mississippi peoples lived in at least nine town settlements that were situated up and down the Mississippi River. These villages of Mound Builders were ruled by a powerful chief called the Great Sun. This ruler lived in the largest of the Natchez settlements, known as the Great Village.

Most of the Mound Builders had vanished by the seventeenth

Some of the earliest occupants of the Mississippi River basin were a group of people called the Mound Builders. The Mississippian Culture of mound builders lived in the area between 900 and 1500 A.D. and constructed earthen pyramids that were temples and dwelling sites for their chiefs. One of the Mound Builders' most important cities, Cahokia, near the site of modern-day St. Louis, had a population of over 25,000 and included 150 mounds, some even 10 stories high. The mounds that remain intact today are preserved at the Cahokia Mounds State Historic Site, shown here.

century, but other tribes of Native Americans could be found along the banks of the Mississippi River. Algonquian-speaking tribes lived on both sides of the river north of the site where the Ohio River flows into the Mississippi. These tribes lived to the north, in the modern-day states of Wisconsin, Illinois, and Minnesota. The Indians in this region included the Sauk and Fox, situated in northern Illinois and Wisconsin. The Kaskaskia, largely an Illinois tribe, lived along the western banks of the

Mississippi River in modern-day Missouri during the 1700s. By the beginning of the 1800s, the Delaware and Shawnee tribes had moved to the Mississippi's west bank, setting up their camps near Cape Girardeau, Missouri.

For tribes living on the Great Plains to the west of the Mississippi, the river served as a natural boundary. After the arrival of the Europeans and the acquisition of the horse by the Lakota, for example, the Mississippi River marked a barrier to these nomadic tribesmen, who were unfamiliar with canoe travel on the river, its tributaries, and the lakes to the east. Southeast of the Ohio–Mississippi confluence, the Native Americans spoke the Muskogean family of languages. These tribes included the Chickasaw, Creek, Choctaw, and Natchez. Along the southern part of the Mississippi River, in Arkansas and Louisiana, the tribes known as the Caddo, Tunica, and Attacapa made their homes.

The majority of these tribes utilized the Mississippi as a trade route, a means of travel, and a source of water. They made little impact on the river itself, choosing to live in harmony with the natural environment in which they lived.

Writer Ann McCarthy sums up the naturalistic, unassuming relationship the Native Americans had with the great Mississippi River before the arrival of Europeans:

> Before the coming of the white man the Mississippi River was a catalyst for a diversified Indian population. They had lived along its banks for countless generations. For the most part, they farmed and lived peacefully in permanent villages between their fields and the river. That the Mississippi might be marketable was inconceivable to the Indians. The river was just there. To call it their own made no more sense than to stake a claim to the forests, mountains or sky. As Indians they revered the spirit of the mighty river, for such a great river could be an enraged enemy, or a trusted friend, but was always comforting as a familiar presence. Above all, the river provided food and a means of transportation.[6]

For hundreds, even thousands, of years, these Native American culture groups remained interconnected because of the Mississippi and other regional rivers. Their canoes kept them in close contact for commerce, diplomacy, and warfare. By the sixteenth century, however, strangers began to arrive in the Indian villages along the banks of the Father of Waters. The same river that had provided food, mobility, security, and productivity for the Native Americans who had chosen their river for their home helped deliver Europeans to their midst. The arrival of these mysterious foreigners would change their world and that of the Mississippi River forever.

The First Europeans

B y the 1500s, nearly all the modern-day Native American tribes were already in existence, including those along the Mississippi River and its tributaries. Those tribal units often competed for resources, hunted on the same lands, fished in the same rivers, and paddled their canoes up and down the same waterways. Often, they considered one another with suspicion and even disdain. Most Indian groups saw themselves as special and considered neighboring tribes different and, therefore, inferior. A neighboring tribe, as well as those located hundreds of miles distant, might only be valued for what unique goods they might have to trade. Tribal conflict was common, and Indian warfare was a frequent activity. In the midst of this whirlwind of Native American contact and conflict, new peoples began to arrive in the New World of North America, including the region watered by the Mississippi River.

Some of the first Europeans to reach the Mississippi River were Spaniards. The Italian mariner Christopher Columbus had sailed across the Atlantic in search of a short, direct route to the Orient and had accidentally bumped into the Western Hemisphere, which contained two continents completely unknown to any Europeans of the fifteenth century. His voyage and others allowed the Spanish monarchy to claim vast territories, including parts of North America, as Spanish-controlled lands. These early Spaniards were intent on exploring throughout the New World in search of new lands and untapped riches and to spread the message of Christianity.

Among the first Europeans to reach the Mississippi was Alonzo Alvarez de Pineda, who arrived at the mouth of the river in 1519. On his map, de Pineda labeled the Mississippi River "Rio del Espiritu Santo"—the River of the Holy Spirit. In 1527, another Spanish explorer, Panfilo de Narvaez, led an expedition up the Mississippi from the Gulf of Mexico along with 300 men. He had heard stories of a rich land to the north—but Narvaez failed to even recognize the mouth of the Mississippi, and many of his men died "beneath the palms and cypresses of the coastal plain or on the bleak refuge of the Texas coast."[7]

More than a decade would pass before another Spanish conquistador reached the Mississippi River north of its mouth. He was a soldier of fortune whose adventures in the New World had earlier taken him to the lands of the Incas of South America, where his commander, Francisco Pizarro, had destroyed the Incan empire and stripped it of its gold. Hernando de Soto led an expedition of more than 700 soldiers and Catholic friars into North America in 1539, landing along the coast of Florida to search for the riches that had eluded Narvaez more than 10 years earlier. De Soto and his men, on meeting their first tribe of Florida Indians, found a long lost survivor of Narvaez's expedition who had spent the previous nine years under the protection of the chief. (The fellow Spaniard looked so much like an Indian that he was almost shot by some of de Soto's men before he could identify himself.) Juan Ortiz became a valuable asset to de Soto, because he could speak several Native American languages.

De Soto traveled across the American Southeast—including land that is now in Georgia, Tennessee, the Carolinas, Alabama, and Mississippi—making contact with several different tribes of Indians, including one in modern-day Georgia, which had a female chief, the Lady of Cafitachequi, who gave de Soto 200 pounds of pearls in exchange for one of his ruby rings. After two years, the Spanish leader reached the banks of the Mississippi on May 8, 1541. One of de Soto's party describes the event:

> He went to see the river and found there . . . an excellently situated land for establishing the camp. It was nearly a half league wide, and if a man stood still on the other side one could not tell whether he were a man or something else. It was of great depth, and of very strong current. Its waters were always turgid and continually many trees and wood came down it, borne along by the force of the current. . . . It had abundance of fish of various kinds and most of them different from those of the fresh waters of Spain.[8]

Although de Soto continued his explorations for another year,

Spaniards were some of the first Europeans to explore the New World, hoping to spread Christianity and find riches. In 1541, Spanish conquistador Hernando de Soto reached the river after two years of exploring what is now the American southeast. The Spanish monarchy did not follow up on his discovery, depicted here in a nineteenth-century drawing, until over a century later.

until his death in May 1542, his claim of the Mississippi on behalf of the Spanish monarch was not followed up for a century and a half. The lure of riches in the Caribbean, Mexico, and South America held the attention of the greedy Spanish. Other Europeans remained equally slow to see the potential wealth of the extensive Mississippi River region that dominated the central portion of North America.

For some time, those Europeans who gave their attention to the Mississippi River during the sixteenth and seventeenth centuries believed that it might hold the key to reaching the Pacific Coast. Since the days of Christopher Columbus, Europeans had searched for an all-water route through the Americas to the Orient, which lay to the distant west. One such European explorer was a Frenchman named Jean Nicolet. In 1634, Nicolet was sent from the Canadian outpost of Quebec by the town's founder, Samuel de Champlain, in search of the route to the west, often called the Northwest Passage. Stories of a great western river inspired men such as Champlain to imagine that its water flowed as far as the Pacific Ocean. Nicolet, along with seven Indian guides, traveled up the Ottawa River; across the Great Lakes to Green Bay, on the west coast of Lake Michigan; and to the Fox River. His expedition marked the farthest any European had ever traveled west across Canada, known then as New France.

As Nicolet traveled, he carried with him "a brightly-colored damask gown with a flower and bird design, so he would be properly attired when he met the Chinese."[9] He did not reach the Orient, however. He did manage to make contact with the Winnebago Indians, who were fearful of his musket, which they believed indicated that Nicolet was a thunder god. Eventually, Nicolet returned to Quebec having failed to find the nonexistent Northwest Passage. In fact, the French explorer never even reached the waters of the Mississippi River.

As the French continued to expand their occupation of North America across Canada and the Great Lakes, other lands beckoned to the west and south. The rewards the French received from these explorations did not include vast riches such as the gold and silver the Spanish had found in Mexico and South America. The French established a New World economy based on extensive trade systems with the Native Americans, especially in furs. In 1661, Louis XIV came to the throne of France. Then a young man barely 21 years old, he set out to increase the power of France not only in Europe, but in the Americas as well. As part of his overall plan, Louis appointed a new Intendant of New France named Jean Talon. He entrusted Talon to increase the level of French involvement in the Indian fur trade. In addition, Talon encouraged Catholic missionaries, usually from the Jesuit order, to immigrate to New France. They were to convert as many Indians as possible to the Christian faith and thereby increase the "Europeanization" of the Native Americans and increase France's grasp on North America.

The Jesuits, dressed in their black robes, were soon scattering across the Great Lakes, concentrating their efforts among the Algonquians in the region where Lakes Huron, Superior, and Michigan come together, near Michilimackinac, Sault Ste. Marie, and Green Bay. It was here that Catholic missionaries began to hear stories of an immense and powerful river to the south, which they called the "Mech-e Se-be."

By 1672, Intendant Talon sent a Jesuit missionary into the region south of the Great Lakes to make contact with additional tribes of Native Americans and to search out the truth of this legendary river. The priest, Father Jacques Marquette, had been working among the Huron and Ottawa Indians at a mission near modern-day Ashland, Wisconsin. Both tribes traded with Indians to the south, including the Illinois. The Illinois told Marquette of a great southern river and of Indians they traded with far downstream who wore necklaces made of glass beads. They also spoke of seeing "great canoes with sails" at the river's mouth, located a great distance to the south. Marquette began to imagine that the "Mech-e Se-be" was a river that flowed clear to the Gulf of Mexico. In his personal journal, he wrote of a plan to travel to this vast interior river:

> If I can get the canoe which the Illinois have promised to make for me, I intend—with some other Frenchmen who can speak with these tribes in their own tongue—to navigate this river and reach those unknown tribes. I then will be able to decide the question of the true direction in which the great river flows.[10]

After receiving all the required permissions from French authorities in Quebec, the capital of New France, Father Marquette; his friend, a trader named Louis Joliet; and five other Frenchmen called voyageurs, or professional boatmen, set off on their mission to the south. Two Indian guides were also included in the small exploring party. The date was May 17, 1673.

Perhaps no pair of traveling companions better than Marquette and Joliet had ever come together in the New World. The French monk was extremely popular with the Great Lakes tribes he encountered, and Joliet was a natural mapmaker. His trading skills made him a favorite of the Native Americans, as well. Joliet was also an extremely brave and fearless man who was not deterred by the Indian stories of great river monsters to the south and of gigantic whirlpools waiting to pull an unsuspecting canoe crew into its grip. As the men paddled their birch-bark canoes, they reached Grande Baie, along the western shore of Lake Michigan. (Later English settlers would call the inlet Green Bay.) They also reached the lands of the Menominee Indians. The French priest recorded in his journal how these Native Americans warned him and his party of fierce Indians to the south "who never show any mercy to strangers, but break their heads without any cause."[11] They also warned of "a demon that was heard from a great distance and barred the way and swallowed up all who ventured to approach."[12] The Frenchmen continued their voyage to the south.

From Green Bay, the party portaged, or carried, their canoes two miles between the Fox and Wisconsin Rivers. Father Marquette named these lands with a name used by the local Indians—"Mesconsing." (The English later called it "Wisconsin.") As they paddled on, the men saw shaggy animals grazing on the prairie grass, which they referred to as "Illinois Oxen clothed in wool." These were American bison, which could still be found east of the Mississippi River in the seventeenth century. After several days of canoeing, they reached the banks of the Upper Mississippi River, at a place located today near Prairie du Chien, Wisconsin. On that day, June 17, 1673, Father Marquette recorded thankful words in his journal: "We safely entered the Mississippi . . . with a Joy that I cannot Express."[13]

By the mid-seventeenth century, France had expanded their occupation of North America through intense exploration and the establishment of a trade system with Native Americans. King Louis XIV also encouraged Catholic missionaries, especially Jesuits, to immigrate to the New World in hopes of promoting the "Europeanization" of Native Americans through conversion and thereby increasing France's grasp on the region. In this painting, two such French explorers, Father Jacques Marquette, a missionary, and his friend Louis Joliet, a trader, are shown on a journey down the Mississippi in 1672.

The Frenchmen continued south, paddling the waters of this enormous river. One of the men took a sounding of the depth of the river using a rope with a lead weight fastened to its end. They discovered that the river was 114 feet deep. Great catfish struck against the sides of their canoes, causing the explorers to jump in surprise. Still, the party proceeded. Along a Mississippi River bank in modern-day Illinois, the intrepid Frenchmen saw frightening artwork on some rocks. Father Marquette described the paintings:

> [We] saw two monsters painted on . . . rocks, which startled us at first, and on which the boldest Indian dares not gaze long. They are as large as a calf, with horns on the head like a deer, a fearful look, red eyes, bearded like a tiger, the face somewhat like a man's, the body covered with scales, and the tail so long that it twice makes the turn of the body . . . these two monsters are so well painted . . . good painters in France would find it hard to do as well.[14]

Just days later, they reached the camps of the Illinois Indians. Here, Father Marquette was given bowls of boiled bear, buffalo, and even dog meat. The Illinois also gave the Jesuit missionary a peace pipe (he had traded with the Illinois at his Great Lakes mission), which he could use as a "passport" when the French encountered other tribes farther south along the river. The Illinois warned Marquette and Joliet of the warlike Shawnee, as well as the Spanish, whom they would encounter on the Lower Mississippi.

For this intrepid crew of Frenchmen, the voyage down the Mississippi was a calm one, the river generally tranquil and inviting. However, when they reached the point where the Missouri River emptied its waters into the Mississippi, the men were greeted by

> the noise of a rapid, into which we were about to run. I have seen nothing more dreadful. An accumulation of large and entire trees, branches, and floating islands, was issuing from the mouth of the river pekistanoui [Missouri] with such impetuosity that we could not without great danger risk passing through it. So great was the agitation that the water was very muddy, and could not become clear.[15]

The monk and the trader continued along the great river as

far south as the site where the Arkansas River flows into the Mississippi. There, with the threat of the Spanish farther south, they decided to turn back, having covered hundreds of miles of the Father of Waters. After a difficult and lengthy voyage back north to New France, Marquette and Joliet returned to Quebec—after logging 2,500 miles of exploration—where they were received enthusiastically as they described the great river they had discovered. The two explorers told French authorities in Quebec of how they had claimed the lands of the Mississippi River on behalf of France and of their knowledge that the great river flows south to the Gulf of Mexico. From their first exploration in search of the Mississippi River, "they gained honor and official recognition of the value of the waterway whose rendezvous with the Gulf of Mexico they had ascertained."[16] In fact, Father Marquette returned to make a second voyage on the Mississippi in 1675 to return to the villages of his friends, the Illinois. Unfortunately, he fell ill and died during the spring voyage.

Despite the honors given to Marquette and Joliet, the explorations they carried out were not followed immediately by other French explorers and traders. One factor that affected long-range French interest in the Mississippi River region was the Canadian winters. During the coldest season of the year, traders in Quebec would use the St. Lawrence River to reach the Great Lakes and the Upper Mississippi. However, the St. Lawrence was typically frozen for five months of the year, limiting French water access to the interior regions of North America. The French eventually realized that to utilize the Mississippi River more effectively, they would have to establish colonies at the mouth of the river, far to the south, and access the river from the Gulf of Mexico.

Seven years would pass until such a French expedition was mounted by a larger group of explorers and settlers led by René-Robert Cavelier, Sieur de La Salle, and the Chevalier Henri de Tonti, a trusted and loyal lieutenant. In January 1682, La Salle set out to explore the Mississippi River with 54 men, including 31 Indians. The French explorer envisioned himself as a type of Spanish conquistador, much like Cortés. La Salle was a strong, energetic man, one of great bravery. Unlike Father Marquette, he was not a gentle man or easy to get along with. He was vain and haughty and had little patience for the failings of others. He was not easy to like.

La Salle intended his exploration of the Mississippi to over-shadow the success of the Marquette and Joliet venture. His original plan called for a large ship weighing 40 tons to be used to travel the Mississippi, but this vessel would have proven too large, impossible to portage from one river to another. Luckily for La Salle, he became impatient with the ship's construction and abandoned it completely, choosing instead to make his trip using canoes similar to those used by the French explorers nearly a decade earlier.

As La Salle traveled across the same region of rivers, bays, and lakes as Marquette and Joliet, he planned to establish permanent outposts, a series of forts to ensure French control of the region. To that end, he founded Fort Crevecoeur in modern-day Illinois, the first European settlement in the area. He established another outpost, Fort Saint Louis, along the Illinois River on his way back up river. As the party reached the Mississippi and floated their canoes south down its endless and meandering route, La Salle did not intend to turn around at the Arkansas River as Marquette and Joliet had done. He was bound to follow the river to the Gulf of Mexico and make additional land claims on behalf of France and its king.

After four months of travel, La Salle and his men did reach the mouth of the Mississippi in April. He claimed the region and named it "Louisiana" after King Louis XIV, stating, "In the name of the most high, mighty, invincible, and victorious Prince Louis the Great . . . I . . . do take possession of this country . . . the seas, harbors, ports, bays, adjacent straits; and all the nations, people, provinces, cities, towns, villages, mines, minerals, fish-eries, streams, [and] rivers."[17] Two years later, he returned to the Mississippi intent on establishing a colony near the river's

RECOVERING A LOST LA SALLE SHIP

Although more than 300 years have passed since La Salle's fateful attempt to launch a French colony along the coast of modern-day Texas, a long-forgotten reminder of that colonizing effort resurfaced in the 1990s.

In 1995, a group of marine archaeologists led by Barto Arnold of the Texas Historical Commission, discovered the remains of a shipwreck in Matagorda Bay off the Texas coast. The wooden remains sat in just 12 feet of water. Closer examination of the wreck revealed the ship to be one of La Salle's four colonizing vessels, which had sunk in January 1686 while the French explorer was sailing along the east Texas coast.

The ship was the *Belle,* the smallest of La Salle's ships. Divers recovered from the wreckage pewter plates, pottery pieces, a stoneware pitcher, sword hilt, brass buckle, bells, and trade goods from the site. When divers uncovered a bronze cannon weighing 700 pounds from the wreck, the 300-year-old gun revealed markings that were identified as the crest of Louis XIV, the French monarch who had dispatched La Salle to the New World with four ships to carry colonists to the mouth of the Mississippi, including the *Belle.*

In the late 1990s, the Texas Historical Commission launched an effort to recover the treasures of the *Belle,* as well as parts of the wreck itself. Because the ship's remains were in shallow water, engineers erected a coffer dam, consisting of "two concentric steel-plate walls that permitted seawater to be pumped away from the wreck,"[*] around the site, exposing it for "dry land" excavation.

Because the *Belle* had sunk while still loaded with a vast cargo of items intended for La Salle's planned colony, archeologists uncovered a huge trove of artifacts, including everyday items such as leather shoes, a wooden crucifix, bronze rings, candlesticks, unopened casks of muskets, and straight pins, many of them well preserved in the mud of Matagorda Bay. Other, more exotic items, included 700,000 blue, white, and black glass beads, brought by the French for trade with the Native Americans. The skeleton of a French soldier was also uncovered.

Conservation of the items found in the *Belle* soon became a major project for the archaeologists involved in their recovery. The La Salle wreck provided historians with a snapshot of the ill-fated expedition, a moment in time preserved in the waters off the coast of Texas. As project director Arnold noted, "La Salle comes alive again. I feel as though I'm reaching across 300 years to shake his hand."[**]

[*] Quoted in Archaeological Institute of America, "Belle Bonanza." *Archaeology*, 27 February 1998. [http://www.archaeology.org/magazine.php?page=online/news/ belle].

[**] Ibid.

mouth. His earlier visit had convinced him of the value of settling the Lower Mississippi Valley:

> We shall obtain everything which has enriched New England and Virginia . . . timber of every kind, salted meat, tallow, corn, sugar, tobacco, honey, wax, resin, and other gums . . . immense pasturages . . . a prodigious number of buffaloes, stags, hinds, roes, bears, otters, lynxes . . . hides and furs . . . there are cotton, cochineal nuts, turnsoles [a variety of plants], . . . entire forests of mulberry trees . . . slate, coal, vines, apple-trees.[18]

He brought along a well-armed, fully supplied contingent of 400 colonists, including women, onboard four ships. La Salle's colonization venture met with immediate problems. One of his ships was captured by Spanish pirates. The French aristocrat mistakenly identified Matagorda Bay, in Texas, as the mouth of the Mississippi. There, the party of colonizers met with fierce Indian opposition. Years passed, and the French colonists clung to their outpost in desperation. By 1687, La Salle realized that he had placed the colony in the wrong location and set out on foot to find the true mouth of the Mississippi. During his search, some dissatisfied colonists turned against him; set out to find their leader, whom they no longer believed in; and murdered him. La Salle died 350 miles away from the Mississippi River he gave his life to colonize. In time, the remaining colonists abandoned their frontier outpost and attempted to return to civilization. With no ship at their disposal, some of the survivors of La Salle's colony reached the Mississippi and walked the entire distance up the river and north until they reached Quebec in New France.

Despite the failure of La Salle's grandiose plans for colonizing the Lower Mississippi in the name of France, others followed and achieved greater success. In 1699, a Frenchman named Pierre le Moyne, Sieur d'Iberville, erected an outpost near modern-day Biloxi, Mississippi, near the mouth of the Mississippi. Iberville further explored the region, traveling upstream as far as the Red River. Iberville returned to France to recruit colonists the following year, but he left his younger brother, Jean Baptiste le Moyne, Sieur de Bienville, in command of the outpost. (The French effort soon paid off when Bienville and his men encountered a group of English explorers intending to travel up the Mississippi. Bienville turned them around at a site today called "the English Turn."[19])

For the next several years, Bienville moved his outpost to the site of present-day Mobile, Alabama, but in time he realized that the best location was at the mouth of the Mississippi itself, which led to his establishment of a colony site called New Orleans in 1718. By 1722, New Orleans was designated as the provincial government capital of the vast region lying west of the Mississippi and claimed by the French called Louisiana. New Orleans was destined, during the eighteenth century, to become the most important port city in North America. French settlement soon followed establishment of these outposts. That same year, a French colonization company was established to send "6,000 white colonists and 3,000 Negro slaves to Louisiana."[20] Up and down the Lower Mississippi River, European settlers arrived to stake their claims. Small agricultural communities were built where French colonists began cultivating sugar and rice in lower Louisiana. In 1719, 200 French miners and 500 slaves arrived upriver in modern-day Missouri to explore for lead deposits.

Not all of the European settlement along the river was French. Hundreds of Germans and other Europeans arrived and took up residence along the river where the Arkansas River empties into the Mississippi, in present-day southeast Arkansas. Throughout these years and until 1742, Bienville remained in the region, serving as governor.

To protect French claims to the region of the Mississippi, the French established defensive forts at strategic locations along the river. Fort Chartres, near Kaskaskia in modern-day southern Illinois, became the capital of the French district of Illinois by 1721. Fort Orleans was established at the mouth of the Osage

River in Missouri. By the 1730s, the French settlements of Sainte Geneviève and New Madrid, along the Mississippi in present-day Missouri, had been established. From such settlement sites, the French regularly carried on trade, especially in furs, with the local tribes of Indians. They established farming communities, shipping their produce down river to the ocean port of New Orleans. Mining operations in places such as Missouri produced valuable quantities of lead. And the extensive presence of the French along the Mississippi served as a limited deterrent to the western migration of frontiersmen from the 13 British colonies along the Atlantic coast.

One of the last of the French outpost settlements was founded in 1764. The previous year, the French and British concluded a treaty ending a war they had fought since the mid-1750s. Under the Treaty of Paris (1763), the French lost all their territorial claims east of the Mississippi, including New France itself. This turn of events caused the French settlers at the old Indian site of Cahokia to surrender their outpost and take residence on the west side of the Mississippi. These French refugees called their new settlement St. Louis. St. Louis remained a small outpost for the remainder of the eighteenth century, but the days of French settlement and colonization in North America were numbered as a new country in North America rose to a position of power and dominance: the United States.

Making
the River
American

The war fought between the British and the French during the 1750s and 1760s, for control of parts of North America, known as the French and Indian War, resulted in tremendous losses for the French in the New World. (The war was part of a larger conflict called the Seven Years' War, which was also fought in Europe.) They not only lost Canada, the Ohio Country, and their claims to the Mississippi River region, they were also forced to surrender ownership of the vast western lands of Louisiana to the Spanish. Even though the French national influence was officially removed from the Mississippi Valley—former French settlements, including their forts, were turned over to the victorious British—the future of the region was soon in the hands of the Americans, who freed themselves from British control during the Revolutionary War (1775–83).

Even before the Revolutionary War, British subjects began moving west across the Appalachian Mountains into the western lands of modern-day Kentucky, Tennessee, Ohio, and Indiana. The growth of the American population during the period from 1790 to 1800 nearly demanded that the new republic look to the west for expansion. Within that decade, the number of Americans increased from 3.9 million to 5.3 million. The frontier deterrent represented by Indians was also largely eliminated by 1795 with the signing of the Treaty of Greenville, which called for the Indians to surrender the southern half of Ohio, plus a small portion of Indiana. That same year, an American diplomat, Thomas Pinckney, negotiated a treaty with the Spanish to open up the Mississippi River for American river traffic and trade. The Spanish had completely closed New Orleans to American river trade between 1784 and 1788. Since 1788, the Spanish had allowed Americans to sell their produce in New Orleans only after they paid customs duties. This new agreement gave Americans the "right of deposit," allowing them to offload their flatboats and river barges and store their produce, without paying a duty, until an American ship arrived to carry the frontier produce to markets overseas.

The Pinckney Treaty was greeted across the trans-Appalachian frontier with great enthusiasm. The Americans on the frontier needed access to the Mississippi River and the Spanish-controlled port of New Orleans for shipping their frontier produce to market. Both of these treaties pointed the Americans not only to the west but also down the Ohio River toward the Mississippi.

Over the next 30 or 40 years, hundreds of thousands of Americans moved into the national interior. They occupied land all the way to the Mississippi River and even farther west. Many of these early emigrants traveled on the same rivers, streams, and lakes that the Native Americans had paddled along for hundreds of years. These western pioneers were mostly farmers, and they grew crops and raised hogs and cattle that needed to be sold. For many of these farmers, the cheapest way to get such goods to market was to float them down the western river system to the great port of New Orleans, located at the mouth of the Mississippi River.

This period of American history, from the 1780s through the great Mississippi steamboat years before the Civil War, saw many different kinds of rivercraft used on the western rivers. Among the earliest and most important types were flatboats and keelboats. These two types of boats carried much of the farm produce raised by Ohio Valley farmers. The first flatboats could be found on the Ohio River. Such a boat was built for rivers, because its flat bottom allowed it to float safely in as little as a few feet of water. A flatboat was not really a boat but a big, floating box, which almost anyone with the right tools could build. It had a rectangular shape, and its sides stood about five feet high. Flatboats came in different sizes, according to their purposes, ranging in length from 20 to 100 feet and were 10 to 25 feet in width. Flatboats were meant to float a farmer's produce downstream only.

The average flatboat could carry lots of western farm produce. As many as 400 to 500 barrels or crates could be crowded on the boat's deck. Items shipped on western flatboats included fruits, vegetables, and livestock such as cattle, chickens, and hogs. Even slaves were shipped downriver to be sold at the markets in

Among the earliest forms of transportation on the Mississippi River, aside from canoes, were flatboats and keelboats, popular from the 1780s until the emergence of steamboats just before the Civil War. Flatboats, like the one shown in this photograph taken in 1898, carried western produce, livestock, and even slaves downstream to New Orleans, where the boats were dismantled and sold as lumber.

Natchez, Mississippi, or New Orleans. When these flatboats reached their downriver destination, they were broken up and sold for the lumber. Many of New Orleans's early sidewalks were built from flatboat lumber. During the early decades of the 1800s, between 400 and 700 flatboats arrived in New Orleans every year. The year 1847 was the busiest for flatboats: More than 2,600 flatboats made the trip from the Ohio River to New Orleans.

Another western rivercraft was the keelboat. This boat was very different from a flatboat, because it was a permanent craft. It was much more expensive to build than a flatboat, costing

DISCOVERING THE SOURCE OF THE MISSISSIPPI RIVER

When the United States gained control of the Mississippi with the purchase of Louisiana from the French, Americans set out in search of the river's source, the site of northern origin for a river that grew in size with each mile it flowed south toward the Gulf of Mexico.

In 1805, as Meriwether Lewis and William Clark were scaling the Rockies with the Corps of Discovery, having already discovered the source of the Missouri River, another American explorer began his search for the source of the Mississippi. Twenty-six-year-old Zebulon Pike, a lieutenant in the U.S. Army, had been ordered to explore the northern regions of the Louisiana Territory. In August of that year, he and 20 other soldiers left St. Louis and set out upriver in a 70-foot-long keelboat, bound for the north country.

Pike and his men traveled as far as Little Falls, Minnesota, before settling into winter quarters. By then, the party had been forced to abandon its keelboat and was traveling by sled up the Mississippi's main branch. In following this course, Pike inadvertently bypassed the true source of the Mississippi. When he finally reached a fur post at Leech Lake, in modern-day Minnesota, Pike declared it "the main source of the Mississippi."[*]

More than 25 years later, another explorer located the true source of the Mississippi. In 1832, Henry P. Schoolcraft, an Indian agent and mineralogist, set out in search of the great river's beginnings. He had participated in a previous expedition in the region in 1820 to find the river's source, but the party had given up their search just three days short of reaching their elusive destination. Twelve years later, Schoolcraft returned to the Minnesota country, securing a local Ojibway chief named Yellow Head as his guide. Schoolcraft wrote in his journal of the moment of discovery: "On turning out of a thicket, into a small weedy opening, the cheering sight of a transparent body of water burst upon our view."[**] On reaching the lake's shore, Schoolcraft bent down, drinking "the limpid cup at the Mississippi's spring."[***]

Schoolcraft had, indeed, found the source of the Mississippi. He named the body of water Lake Itasca, which he derived by combining two Latin words, *verITAS* and *CAput,* which translate as "truth" and "head." The intrepid explorer was so thrilled at his discovery that he wrote a poem in honor of the great river whose source had remained elusive for so many centuries to Europeans and Americans alike:

> Ha! Truant of western waters who hast
> So long concealed thy very sources—flitting shy,
> Now here, now there—through spreading mazes vast
> Thou art, at length, discovered to the eye.[+]

[*] Quoted in Tom Weil, *The Mississippi River*, 27.
[**] Ibid., 26.
[***] Ibid.
[+] Ibid.

between $2,000 and $3,000. Keelboats had "professional" crews that carried western goods downriver for a fee. Typically, a keelboat could deliver a ton of cargo upriver cheaper than the cargo could be carried overland by wagon.

A keelboat was built with a four-inch-square strip of timber called a keel running from bow to stern. The boats were generally 60 to 70 feet long and featured a cargo hold three or four feet deep. The boats were pointed at both the bow and the stern. A box-shaped cabin covered the center of the deck. Keelboats usually had a center mast with a sail. Most keelboats required a crew of about 10.

On each side of the keelboat's deck was a walkway where the crew could "pole" the boat upriver. To do this, each person would take a turn pushing a long pole into the river bottom and "walking" the boat upstream. These setting poles were usually about 12 to 14 feet long and capped with iron. Cleats were nailed across the walkway to give the polers something to push against as they walked. If the river current was too strong, the crew was forced to "cordelle" the boat. In this method, the crew used long ropes tied to a tree onshore and pulled the boat upstream.

The Mississippi River became such an important highway for American commerce during the 1790s that some Americans, especially Thomas Jefferson, who was elected as America's third president in 1800, began considering the possibilities of a permanent American presence in the region. Some became convinced that the future of the great American West beyond the river, the Trans-Mississippi West, was destined to become part of the United States. Once president, Jefferson began inquiring about the possibility of the United States government purchasing the port of New Orleans, creating an American center of western commerce.

The same year Jefferson was elected chief executive, a secret treaty between the Spanish and the French changed ownership of the vast Louisiana region, control of the Lower Mississippi River, and of the port of New Orleans back to France. The Treaty of San Ildefonso was intended as a secret, having been forced on the

Napoleon's quest for power threatened the United States when the leader ordered the port of New Orleans closed to American traffic, hoping to restore French strength in the region. President Thomas Jefferson decided immediate action was necessary in order to protect American interests, and he sent delegates to France to negotiate the purchase of New Orleans and some surrounding land. Surprisingly, the French offered the delegates the entire tract of Louisiana for $15 million and they accepted, as depicted in this painting.

Spanish by Napoleon Bonaparte, the military leader of France, who had taken control of the Spanish monarchy through his military campaigns. Jefferson soon became aware of the planned transfer and faced immediate questions concerning Napoleon's plans in North America. The French general had developed plans to restore French power in the region. To challenge the presence of the Americans in New Orleans, Napoleon ordered the closing of the port of New Orleans to American traffic. Although Spanish officers were still in charge of New Orleans, it was the French who were pulling the strings in the region.

President Thomas Jefferson's purchase of the Louisiana Territory from France in 1803 added 825,000 square miles to the United States. After this purchase, the Mississippi was free from the meddling of other countries and was no longer just a western border but a geographical asset, acting as the main highway for western migration, trade, and transportation.

When Jefferson viewed the troublesome turn of events on his nation's western border, he became convinced that the United States must act quickly and decisively. He sent James Monroe, an American diplomat and close friend, to France to help negotiate the purchase of the port of New Orleans and a portion of West Florida for $10 million. (Congress, however, had only authorized $2 million.)

Monroe and his negotiating partner, Robert Livingston, finally sat down with French officials and were soon stunned when the French offered to sell not only New Orleans but instead the entire tract of Louisiana. The French set the price at $15 million, and the two American negotiators were uncertain how to proceed. They were without instructions to spend $15 million and were not authorized to buy Louisiana! Not wanting to pass up a bargain, however, the two envoys signed a treaty authorizing the Louisiana Purchase on April 30, 1803.

Almost three months passed before President Jefferson received word of the deal from across the Atlantic. In October, Congress ratified the treaty, adding more than 825,000 square miles of western territory to the United States. The purchase was a momentous success for the Jefferson administration, one that set the course for greater western expansion. No longer was the Mississippi River the western boundary of the young American republic. With the purchase and the acquisition of such a vast western tract, one that stretched all the way to the Rocky Mountains, the Mississippi became an even greater geographical asset. Along with such rivers as the Ohio and the Missouri, it would serve as the primary highway for western migration, as well as a jumping-off place for those intrepid Americans who wished to establish their futures on the Great Plains and in the Far West.

Days of Steam

With the acquisition of the Louisiana Territory west of the Mississippi River, Americans were certain of the future of the Mississippi River. They were in control of the river for the first time, and the threat of the river being cut off by the French, Spanish, British, or any other European power had been eliminated. The Mississippi became a more important river for the United States than ever before. Within four years of the purchase, a completely new kind of rivercraft had been invented, one that would change the value of the Mississippi and all other navigable rivers in the country. That new rivercraft was the steam-powered paddle-wheel boat.

The first successful steamboats in America were built back east along the Hudson River plying their courses up and down the river from Albany, the capital of New York, to New York City, one of the great East Coast harbors of the era. This new form of rivercraft soon found its way to the Mississippi River.

Robert Fulton, one of the greatest American inventors, built and launched his *Clermont* in 1807, less than a year after Lewis and Clark returned from their western explorations. In just a few short years, the steamboat proved to be practical, innovative, and commercially viable. As Americans were pouring west by the thousands, it did not take long before Fulton was ready to take his transportation innovation to the West. Fulton joined in this venture with two partners: Robert Livingston, a well-known New York political figure (he had signed the Declaration of Independence back in 1776) and entrepreneur, and Nicholas J. Roosevelt. (Two of his descendents, Theodore and Franklin Roosevelt, later became U.S. presidents.)

Roosevelt's construction of the first western river steamboat began in 1810. Nicholas J. Roosevelt laid the keel for his boat in the summer of 1810, near the frontier town of Pittsburgh, at the headwaters of the Ohio River, where the Monongahela and the Allegheny Rivers join together to form the great western-flowing artery that flows into the Mississippi River. The boat was launched a year later, in March 1811. When Roosevelt finished his boat, it was a side-wheeler, meaning

American inventor Robert Fulton built the first commercially successful steamboat, the *Clermont*, in 1807 on the Hudson River. This steam-powered paddlewheel boat was both practical and commercially successful, revolutionizing transportation and trade along America's rivers.

that the paddle wheel that propelled the boat along the river was built on the side of the boat. Roosevelt's wife christened their paddle-wheel steamboat *New Orleans*. Critics of Roosevelt's boat called it a "dainty teakettle," and predicted that the boat would be no match for the rough river ahead and the equally tough men who made their living—both legally and illegally—along the river.[21]

On September 10, 1811, the Roosevelts began their trip down the Ohio, bound for the Mississippi and the port of New Orleans. In December, the *New Orleans* reached the Mississippi

River. Despite the challenges the Roosevelts and their crew faced on the Mississippi, the underpowered *New Orleans* managed to make it down river and arrive at its Louisiana port city namesake on January 12, 1812. The boat's arrival in New Orleans heralded a serious change in the future of the Mississippi River. As Roosevelt's steamboat passed Natchez, Mississippi, one elderly black man, the slave of a planter named Samuel Davis, standing along the riverbank watched as the boat chugged by and commented, "Ole Mississippi done met her master now!" [22] This early venture to bring steam power to America's largest river paved the way for others to follow in its wake.

One of the first was a western river steamer called the *Comet*, built in 1813 outside Brownsville, Pennsylvania, on the Ohio River. The *Comet* made the trip down river to New Orleans the next year. Its legacy was cut short after only two trips to Natchez, when it was dismantled and her engine sold for use in a southern cotton factory. In 1814, a new design for a steamboat was built by a flatboat operator named Henry M. Shreve. Shreve had spent years in the river trade, serving as a raft pilot before building his own steamboat. Shreve's design included several key innovations. Unlike the *New Orleans,* Shreve's boat was flat-bottomed. He also installed a high-pressure steam engine onboard his vessel, knowing that it would be necessary to make the return trip back up the Mississippi. He also put his steam engine and boiler on the main deck (because there was no "belowdecks" on this shallow draft model), built another deck on top of the first, and placed a pilothouse above that so he could have a panoramic view of the river as he piloted his new craft. Shreve named his boat the *Washington,* after America's first president.

In the spring of 1815, he launched his boat, steaming his way past Louisville, Kentucky, down the Ohio to the Mississippi and New Orleans without significant incident. Then he returned up the two rivers, making Louisville and completing his round trip in 45 days. This time cut down a Louisville–New Orleans round trip to one-third of the time required by keelboat (four to five months). Soon, others were copying Shreve's design for a Mississippi–Ohio steamboat, and the model continued to be used for another century for boats with flat bottoms, shallow draft, two decks, and a pilothouse perched above it all, with glass windows on all four sides and a large wheel for steering.

The first paddle-wheel steamboats were extremely simple, even basic, designs and were fairly crude and unsightly. The early models were often less than 100 feet in length, typically just 50 to 70 feet, and were almost entirely utilitarian. There were few elements included that could be called luxurious or ornate. The main or lower deck of these first steamboats housed the engine equipment, including the steam boilers and the engines themselves. This deck also held the boat's fuel compartments, where chopped wood was stored for burning in the boat's furnace. This deck was typically used to store cargo and other freight. The boat's second deck was usually called the boiler deck, because it was above the boiler. Here, the boat's passengers were assigned rooms for their private use. This deck included the main cabin, where passengers took their meals and otherwise socialized, playing cards, holding dances, recitals, or enjoying other activities. The passenger staterooms lined up on both sides of the boat. The term "stateroom" was applied to the rooms on steamboats because they were often named after states in the Union: Virginia, Ohio, Georgia, and others. The staterooms on early steamboats were usually rows of exposed bunks featuring mattresses stuffed with hay or corn husks. A curtain was drawn in front of each bunk to create a limited amount of privacy. Not until the 1840s did steamboat staterooms became private places with walls and doors. They were also enlarged later. Early staterooms were only about six feet square. Later rooms varied in size, with some extremely spacious and elaborately decorated, where the single bunk was replaced by full-sized beds with soft feather mattresses.

The third deck was an open-sided level where passengers could pass the time outdoors getting the best view of the river and the surrounding countryside. Railings around the outer deck kept the passengers safe. This upper level was called the hurricane deck. Perched above everything else—except the boat's tall black smokestacks—was the smaller fourth deck, where the captain and his officers guided the boat up and down their watery courses. It was called the Texas deck, because Texas became a state just about the time that the upper wheelhouse came into existence. From here, the steamboat pilot commanded a full view of the river and all other traffic coming and going. The main feature of the Texas deck was the giant wheel connected through a series of ropes to the boat's rudder and used to turn the boat to the left or right (port or starboard). From the Texas deck, the pilot could communicate with the engine crew belowdecks through a megaphone system and order up more steam to increase the speed of the boat or a release of steam to slow down.

The steamboats, with their high-pressure engines, burned large quantities of wood. The paddle-wheelers often stopped twice daily at river bank woodyards to restock their wood compartments with cured quantities of such hardwoods as oak, hickory, chestnut, beech, and ash. Such wood sold for between $1.50 and $3.00 a cord. These boats could burn as much as 20 to 30 cords of wood each full day of travel. By the 1840s, so much wood had been cut out of the forests near the riverbanks that the steamboats began switching over to more efficient fuels, coal in particular.

Passage on a Mississippi steamboat in the early days of such travel might cost between $3 for passengers willing to sleep outside on the boat's decks and $15 for a private cabin. Those who chose to take passage on deck often found sleeping diffi-cult, because the steamers often stopped for wood, took on and offloaded cargo, or were otherwise busy places with lots of deck activity. Deck passengers were required to provide their own food. They sometimes paid a little less than the going price for passage if they agreed to help with work, such as loading wood during one of the regular "wooding up" stops. Ironically, steamboat tickets continued to decrease in price as the amenities onboard improved. By 1880, riverboat passage cost about 3¢ per mile, including meals. Traveling from St. Paul, Minnesota, to St. Louis, Missouri, might cost no more than $20.

Along the Ohio–Mississippi River frontiers, early steamboating was less than glamorous. Later models were known for and advertised serving meals on fine china and also such fancy adornments as crystal chandeliers, plush carpets, and richly carved European furniture. The first steamboats, however, were crowded, boisterous, dirty modes of transportation. Passenger fares were low enough to attract a lower class of people, so manners were often crude and lacking in civility. The early engines were noisy and placed too close to the sleeping accommodations. The boats were hot in the summer and cold in the winter. Service onboard such boats was often lacking. A typical early steamboat meal consisted of little more than pork and beans because the boat's cooks might be incapable of serving up any kind of fare worth eating. The water brought to a dining table was usually river water—cloudy, silty, and sometimes thick with mud. Lighting on the early steamboats was little more than candles or kerosene lamps. After the Civil War, steamboats were lit by gas, and electricity came shipboard by the 1870s.

By 1840, Mississippi River steamboating had reached its heyday. For the next 20 years, until the opening of the Civil War, the conditions on river steamers improved and the number of steamboats increased to the highest levels in history. Boats began to boast the best food, luxurious sleeping accommodations, and excellent service. Among the most elaborately decorated and ornate steamboats were the *Natchez, Robert E. Lee, Grand Republic,* and *J.M. White.* The latter was a side-paddle boat built in 1878, and it had the reputation for being the fastest boat on the Mississippi. The *J.M. White* was longer than a football field and was festooned with steamboat gothic woodwork, sleek black chimneys capped with wrought-iron featherwork. As fancy as this elegant boat was outside, inside it was a floating palace. Historian Ron Larson describes the interior of the *J.M. White*:

> On each side of the grand saloon were rows of elegant state rooms. Overhead were stained glass windows. The ceiling was supported by ornate columns and connecting arches carved in lacelike patterns. The grand saloon was carpeted with rich thick Brussels carpeting and illuminated by crystal chandeliers equipped with gas lamps. The walls were paneled in walnut or rosewood. Handsome upholstered and hand-carved furniture was used throughout the grand saloon. There was a grand piano and a large silver water cooler with silver drinking cups chained to its sides.[23]

As elaborate as the *J.M. White* was as it plied the waters of the Mississippi, its service on the river only lasted eight years. In December 1886, a fire erupted in the boat's boiler room on the main deck. In no time, the boat was engulfed in flames, and it burned to the waterline, as yet another elegant lady of the river lost to mechanical calamity.

Between 1811 and 1850, approximately 4,000 steamboats became casualties of the river. In some cases, the boat was destroyed by an explosion when unchecked boilers overheated. Others became victims of the river itself, when their shallow draft hulls were torn by tree branches, or snags, that had fallen or floated into the river. Along one stretch of the river—between Cairo, Illinois, and St. Louis—the channel was so dangerous that river pilots referred to it as "The Graveyard." By 1867, at least 133 riverboats had wrecked in this stretch of difficult Mississippi water. The Mississippi River during those years was a natural river, one that altered its own channels and was often cluttered with dangerous debris and submerged obstacles.

Explosions on steamboats were so common on the Mississippi and other American rivers that legislation was passed requiring greater safety measures on boats. In 1852, Congress passed the Steamboat Act. This piece of legislation required steamboat companies and owners to "correct the unsatisfactory conditions on river paddlewheel steamboats."[24] The law forced steamboat operators to install adequate gauges and other safety equipment on boilers. It also established a licensing program for steam engineers and river pilots.

When the Civil War began in 1861, approximately 1,000 steamboats were in active service on the Mississippi River. Of that number, approximately one-third plied the waters of the Upper Mississippi from St. Louis to St. Paul, Minnesota. During the intervening half-century since Roosevelt's first trip down the Mississippi in the *New Orleans,* regular steamboat service on the river had become commonplace. The first large-scale steamboat service was the Ohio and Mississippi Mail Line, organized out of Louisville, Kentucky, in 1832. The line ran 16 steamboats and delivered mail three times a week downriver to New Orleans. By 1846, regular steamboat service was running from the Ohio River to Memphis, Tennessee, making weekly trips. One company ran four boats between Memphis and New Orleans regularly by 1844. By 1851, from only one company, "three boats tried departures every four days from Louisville for New Orleans."[25] Others joined these numbers, so that by 1859, an additional two lines of regular steamboat service were running from cities on the Ohio to New Orleans.

On the Upper Mississippi, the first steamboat traveled north from St. Louis and reached St. Paul, Minnesota, in 1823. The *Virginia* delivered supplies to Fort Anthony (later called Fort Snelling), where the Minnesota River flows into the Mississippi. Regular scheduled steamboat service on the Upper Mississippi began in 1842 with the arrival of the St. Louis and Keokuk Packet Line. By 1865, this line was running a dozen steamboats on the Upper Mississippi. By 1869, the Northern Line Packet Company operated 20 steamboats between St. Louis and St. Paul. Two years later, the two companies merged and formed the Keokuk Northern Line. A decade later, the line went out of business after the death of its owner, John S. McCune.

In 1881, the St. Louis and St. Paul Packet Company was established, and other companies followed—but the grand era of the

Upper Mississippi steamboats had nearly run its course. Although St. Paul witnessed 1,058 steamboat arrivals at its wharves in 1855, less than 20 years later, only about 200 steamboat arrivals were tallied. The last of the Upper Mississippi River paddle-wheel steamboat packet companies in operation between St. Louis and St. Paul was the Diamond Jo Line, which operated out of Dubuque, Iowa. As late as 1889, the Diamond Jo Line included five steamboats that carried passengers almost exclusively. Most of the freight trade had gone to the railroads by then. By 1911, the line ran only four steamers. That year, the line's owner, Captain Jo, sold his boats to the Streckfus Line in St. Louis. Soon, the boats were remodeled into floating dance-halls and operated as excursion boats during the summer. The days when steamboats epitomized the economic livelihood of the Mississippi River had long since faded away.

During the steamboat era, river traffic did not run every month of the year but rather seasonally and according to the navigability of the Mississippi and Ohio Rivers. The spring rainy season, accompanied by western snowmelt, translated into good water for running the Mississippi. Steamboats could make regular runs with no restrictions. By June, the river faced low-water conditions as the river levels moved up and down, until the fall, when rains were common once again, bringing an increase in river traffic. By November, ice on the river was a problem, and navigation on the Mississippi, Ohio, Missouri, and other rivers dropped significantly or closed down completely.

Those who worked on the steamboats of the early nineteenth century were a unique work force, and nearly everyone onboard steamers, from the captain down to the deckhands, known as roustabouts, were viewed by the river-going public with high regard. To keep a steamboat in operation and in competition with other steamers required several different types of steamboat workers. At the pinnacle of prestige and authority was the boat's captain. He usually owned his own boat and made it his business to keep in touch with nearly every aspect of the boat's operation. He checked the machinery and paid the fuel and repair bills; ordered food for the boat's galley, or kitchen; and provided goods and freight for his boat to carry up and down the river.

The captain had to organize the business end of the steamboat, and the boat's pilot had his own unique responsibilities. If the captain had to know everything about his boat, the pilot had to know everything about the river itself. It was in the river that constant danger lurked, and the pilot had to know the best way to navigate at every turn and bend in the river. He had to memorize the thousands of river channels, know where to make crossings to the deeper water, and know how to spot sandbars, snags, and sawyers—logs or trees that were stuck in the river, presenting a hazard to river traffic. In his book *Life on the River,* historian Norbury L. Wayman describes the significant role played by steamboat pilots:

> His constant vigilance was needed in dangerous waters, where a slight inattention could lead to an accident. . . . The pilot's education was gained through actual practice and observation of the river. Some were licensed only for certain stretches of the steams, those with which they were familiar. His knowledge required learning the myriad details of water depth, current speed, configuration of river bed, and location of snags and other obstacles.[26]

From his high perch in the boat's Texas deck, the pilot remained in verbal contact with the engine room belowdecks, informing the engineer in the boiler room about the appropriate speed for the vessel at every part of the river. Working alongside the engineer was the engine crew, men who worked in the heat of belowdecks, monitoring the heavy machinery and stoking the great boat furnaces with additional fuel. Among the engine crew were stokers, often free blacks, who fed wood or coal into the furnace fires with shovels. Their job was an intense, sweaty, and backbreaking one. On larger boats, there might be as many as 10 boilers, all providing the needed high-pressure steam to keep the steamboat moving along the highway of commerce, the Mississippi River.

Up on the decks, the steamboat crew included those men who carried cargo on and off the steamer. Known as roustabouts, they carried hundreds of crates, barrels, and bales of freight every day. They could find rest only between stops along the river, but when the steamer tied at a new site, the roustabouts were to be up and lively, ready to complete their labors quickly to help keep the steamboat on its posted schedule. To make certain the roustabouts did not shirk their work, the steamboat employed a worker called a mate. This man was a hard driver, one who yelled and taunted his roustabouts to work faster and keep busy at each stop. His voice often could be heard above the mechanical sounds of the boats engines and other machinery as he verbally browbeat his workers to carry their weight.

Pilots relied on one roustabout particularly, a deckhand known as a leadsman. The leadsman was summoned on deck when the pilot tapped a big bell. It was the leadsman's job to let the pilot know the depth of the water the boat was passing over. The roustabout then tossed a rope into the water with a lead weight attached to its end, with which the leadsman took a river sounding, providing the depth. This let the pilot know whether the channel he was following was deep enough for the steamboat to follow it. The soundings were signaled to the pilot through a list of special terms equal to specific depths, such as "mark one" (6 feet of water), "quarter less one" (4½ feet), "quarter twain" (13½ feet), and "quarter one" (7½ feet). Of course, the most famous cry of the leadsman was "mark twain," meaning two fathoms (12 feet) of water, which was considered a safe water depth for steamboats.

The great nineteenth-century writer Samuel Clemens, from the Mississippi River town of Hannibal, Missouri, took the pen name "Mark Twain." Twain wrote some of the best-loved fiction works in American literature, including *The Adventures of Tom Sawyer, The Adventures of Huckleberry Finn* and *Life on the Mississippi,* a book about his own experiences on the Mississippi while working as a riverboat pilot. Twain included a view of the steamboat era in yet another of his novels, *Pudd'nhead Wilson,* which was published in 1894:

> Steamboats passed up and down every hour or so. Those belonging to the little Cairo line and the little Memphis line always stopped; the big Orleans liners stopped for hails only, or to land passengers or freight; and this was the case also with the great flotilla of "transients." These latter came out of a dozen rivers—the Illinois, the Missouri, the Upper Mississippi, the Ohio, the Monongahela, the Tennessee, the Red River, the White River, and so on; and were bound every whither and stocked with every imaginable comfort or necessity which the Mississippi's communities could want, from the frosty Falls of St. Anthony down through nine climates to torrid New Orleans.[27]

With the development of extensive steamboat traffic on the Mississippi during the first half of the nineteenth century, several towns and cities on the river became important stops, as well as significant regional outposts. The greatest city on the Mississippi was always New Orleans. When the Americans bought the Louisiana Territory from the French in 1803, New Orleans was nearly a century old. During the heyday of riverboat traffic, New Orleans mushroomed in size, becoming the leading port in the United States, surpassing even New York City. In 1801, the value of the goods passing through the port of New Orleans was less than $4 million in value. By 1850, nearly $100 million worth of goods were being shipped through the Delta City. During the 1840s, New Orleans handled twice the goods that passed through the port of New York.

Another important Mississippi River city was Natchez, Mississippi. Another French settlement founded in the early 1700s, Natchez became the first important stop for steamboats as they paddled upriver from New Orleans. During the decades before the Civil War, Natchez became a leading cotton port on the Mississippi, making local planters prosperous. Many

Steamboat traffic crowded the Mississippi River by the 1840s and 1850s. Steamboats provided jobs, transported passengers, carried millions of dollars worth of goods, and contributed to the growth and prosperity of many cities along the river's banks. They even provided entertainment at times, as seen in this 1866 engraving of riverboats racing.

steamboats, as well as flatboats, stopped at Natchez while traveling downriver bound for New Orleans.

North of Natchez, along Tennessee's banks of the Mississippi, was the city of Memphis. This southern river town also became a dominant center of the Mississippi River trade in cotton and slaves. Slave traders delivered their slaves upriver from New Orleans and sold them to local plantation owners at Memphis. By 1860, Memphis was an important river town of 23,000 people, making it the sixth-largest community in the south.

Vicksburg, Mississippi, located south of Memphis and north of Natchez, was another significant river town for the cotton trade. By the 1870s, however, the city faced an uncertain future. Vicksburg had been established on high bluffs overlooking the

Mississippi, but by 1876, the river had changed course, creating an oxbow curve and leaving Vicksburg stranded three miles from the river it had been founded and grown up on. Steamboats could no longer tie up at docks along the Vicksburg shore. To solve the problem, the U.S. Army Corps of Engineers altered the course of the Yazoo River to flow by Vicksburg. Because the Yazoo drained into the Mississippi, Vicksburg became a river town with a second life.

Other significant towns and cities also grew on the Upper Mississippi. Yet another early French community, St. Louis, became a key port on the river. Established as a trading post in 1764 by a French trader named Pierre Laclede, St. Louis prospered and grew after the Americans acquired it in 1803. The first steamboat reached the river town in 1817, and St. Louis soon became the "Gateway to the Northwest." By 1840, St. Louis had a population of 16,000 citizens. In another 20 years, its populations had 10 times that number. In 1880, St. Louis was a booming river metropolis of 350,000 people. St. Louis was always an important steamboat town, because dozens of riverboats regularly tied up at its extensive warehouse–wharf. In 1849, a dramatic steamboat disaster occurred when a fire broke out on the paddle-wheel steamboat *White Cloud* while it was tied up at the wharf. The flames jumped to other nearby boats, and before the blaze was over, 23 steamboats were on fire. When the fire reached the warehouses, townspeople used dynamite to blow up buildings in the fire's path, stopping the spread of the blaze.

Farther upriver, other Mississippi towns—Hannibal, Missouri; Keokuk, Iowa; Nauvoo, Illinois; the Quad Cities (Davenport, Iowa, and Rock Island, Moline, and East Moline, Illinois); Dubuque, Iowa; LaCrosse, Wisconsin; and Minneapolis–St. Paul, Minnesota—all left their mark on the river trade.

5

A River Vexed
by War

At the height of the Mississippi steamboat era, the United States became engulfed in a bloody civil war, a conflict that split the nation in two and caused many southern states to attempt to leave the Union, primarily over the issue of the expansion of slavery. For four years, from April 1861 to April 1865, Union forces fought the soldiers of the Confederate States of America. Before the conflict was over, more than 600,000 men in uniform would die. Looking at a map, the Confederate states were generally surrounded by water, including the Atlantic Ocean to the east, the Gulf of Mexico to the south, and the Ohio River to the north. To the west, the Mississippi River divided the states of Arkansas, Louisiana, and Texas from the remainder of the Confederacy. As northern commanders established their overall war strategy for pursuing the war, they included two goals: 1) the eventual establishment of a solid blockade from Chesapeake Bay, south around Florida, and then along the Gulf of Mexico to Texas, and 2) the capture of the Mississippi River.

If the Union could control this highly navigable river, it could split off Texas, Louisiana, and Arkansas from the remainder of the Confederacy. The result of General Winfield Scott's two-tier strategy, called the Anaconda Plan, was to surround the Confederacy geographically and then tighten control of the South much as a snake might surround and squeeze its prey to death. Although Union commanders never surrendered an additional strategy of marching on and capturing the Confederate capital of Richmond, Virginia, the Anaconda Plan was generally followed throughout the war. Therefore, some of the most important and decisive action of the Civil War was centered on controlling the Mississippi River.

Although the Union navy was small when the war opened in the spring of 1861, by year's end, the Federal, or Union, navy had expanded to 260 warships, including newly designed vessels made of iron. These unique boats helped determine the outcome of the war on the Mississippi River and other rivers.

Of the military innovations of the Civil War, perhaps none changed the nature of naval warfare more than the invention of the ironclads—the refitted rivercraft that were sheathed in iron plate, causing cannonballs to bounce off their thick hides. Most ironclads had plating at least four inches thick, usually consisting of two layers of two-inch sheathing. They were steam-powered boats, armed with several cannons.

Before the end of the war, the Union navy had launched 42 ironclads for use as inland rivercraft and as ocean-going vessels. Twenty-two of the Union ironclads were used on various rivers, including the Mississippi, Arkansas, Red, Tennessee, Cumberland, and Ohio. Union forces also captured Confederate ironclads, including the *Tennessee* and the *Atlanta,* and used them as Federal vessels. By the end of the war, the Confederacy had begun construction on 59 ironclads but only finished 24 of the armored ships. Many of the southern ironclads were built by converting wooden frigates and placing iron plate over them, but Union ironclads were generally built from scratch as new vessels.

Major victories in the Mississippi River Valley, including Union General Ulysses S. Grant's victory at Shiloh, Tennessee, in the spring of 1862, were extremely important for the Union's effort to take control of the Mississippi River. Other Union actions were making additional headway toward the goal of the Anaconda Plan: to cut off the western Confederate states of Arkansas, Louisiana, and Texas from the remainder.

Union Major General John Pope launched an offensive in the spring of 1862 to consolidate Union positions on the major water highway. A Federal fleet known as the Western Flotilla included more than 100 river vessels. This "river navy," which included armored steamboats called "turtles," was under the command of Flag Officer Andrew Foote.

Operating from the North and moving slowly downstream, the Union river forces took control of the Mississippi slowly but in a coordinated fashion. One of the goals for early 1862 was the capture of Island No. 10. Located along a hairpin curve in the river near the Missouri Bootheel, the island had a Confederate fortress with about 50 cannons. This fortification was a formidable blockade for Union traffic. The problem for the Union

One of the Union's main goals in the Civil War was to control the Mississippi River. This Union strategy was aided by a military innovation, the ironclad ship, a type of rivercraft fitted with at least four inches of iron plating. By the end of the war the Union had launched 42 ironclads, such as the USS *St. Louis* shown anchored on the Mississippi at the center of this 1862 photograph, while the Confederacy had only constructed 24.

forces was how to approach the island. It was situated toward the lower extremity of a sharp U-shaped curve in the river. North of the island, the land between the two sides of the "U" was thick with low-lying bayous and swamps. Pope believed that if a water route through the bayous could be cleared, troop transports could be sent through and land on the eastern bank of the Mississippi, bypassing Island No. 10 completely.

Federal engineers did cut a new channel. Called "Pope's Canal," it was 50 feet wide, 9 miles long, and less than 5 feet deep. Even then, once Union boats made their way through the swamp, enemy cannon emplacement on the east bank could open fire and destroy them. In addition, Union gunboats would be unable to pass through the cleared swamp channel, because they sat too low in the water.

Despite the doubts of his fellow officers, Commander Henry Walke volunteered to take his gunboat, *Carondelet,* past enemy guns to reach Pope's army and give it support. Walke received permission to make the deadly run. He had a barge filled with coal and hay to catch shells fired from the shore lashed to the port side of his vessel.

During the night of April 4, as frequent flashes of lightning lit up the southern sky, Walke and his men made the run. Shelling was constant, but the enemy fire proved inaccurate and the *Carondelet* completed the gauntlet of Confederate assault in one piece. With a Union gunboat to face, Confederate shore batteries fell one after another. Pope's troops were able to cross the river north of Island No. 10, making the river post impossible to hold. The garrison surrendered to Pope on April 8. Among those present were three Rebel generals.

This important victory eliminated yet another Confederate-fortified bottleneck on the Mississippi, allowing Union troops to move farther downstream. Once Island No. 10 was neutralized, additional Confederate river forts, including Fort Pillow, surrendered. Fort Pillow was a Rebel garrison facing a withering bombardment launched by Federal navy forces that fired 13-inch shells into the Confederate stronghold.

In early May, Flag Officer Foote left the region, having wrestled unsuccessfully with wounds he had received during the siege of Fort Donelson earlier in the year (he died just over a year later). He was followed in command by Flag Officer Charles H. Davis. Davis was in command when the Rebel River Defense Fleet attacked Union gunboats at Fort Pillow on May 10. Eight Confederate vessels launched an assault against the Union crafts, including *Mound City* and *Carondelet.* The Rebel force was defeated, and Davis set his eyes on Memphis, which he took on June 6, after a battle that lasted just over an hour. Each such victory further consolidated Union control of the central length of the Mississippi River.

As the North tightened its hold on the Mississippi, the southern-held port of New Orleans, located at the river's mouth, was slowly being put out of business. River traffic, which had included hundreds of steamboats plying their produce up and down the river from the "Crescent City," was shut off from access to the immense port. New Orleans's docks became deserted, and storage warehouses were closed.

New Orleans was strategically situated for the South. It was the largest city in the seceded states, whose normal trade included shipping to the Caribbean. The North understood the value of taking control of the city. Control of the Mississippi would mean little for either side if that control did not extend to include the city of New Orleans. Approximately 10,000 Confederates held the city, hoping to protect it from a Union invasion that everyone knew would one day come. Most of the defense of the city was actually centered in the forts located to the south. The Mississippi River flowed 100 miles past New Orleans, and several forts, primarily Fort Jackson and Fort St. Philip, provided protection from any Federal force approaching from the Gulf of Mexico.

Fort Jackson was a strong outpost, a star-shaped, stone-and-masonry fort bristling with 74 cannons. Fort St. Philip was also built of stone and brick and held 52 guns. Seven hundred men were stationed in the two forts. A long length of chain extended into the Mississippi from Fort Jackson, a boom that could be raised and lowered to allow friendly river traffic while keeping the enemy out of New Orleans. The chain had log rafts and boat hulks attached to it to further impede an unwanted vessel. In addition, Rebel gunboats, such as the *Louisiana,* were on patrol in the river's waters. Despite this southern blockade of the Mississippi River's entrance, northern forces began moving on the city of New Orleans in 1862. Ship Island, situated in the Gulf near the Mississippi coast, had fallen into Federal hands as early as September 1861. This provided a base for later Union actions against New Orleans.

The Union leader chosen to lead an attempt to capture New Orleans was Flag Officer David G. Farragut. This long-time veteran of the U.S. Navy, who had entered the navy 50 years earlier, at age nine, brought a world of experience to the situation. He had fought in the War of 1812, encountered pirates on the high seas, and seen action in the Mediterranean. Although he had retired to his estate in New York, he went back in uniform when the war broke out.

Operating from Ship Island, the strategy against New Orleans was to move up the Mississippi's lower reaches in wooden ships. Farragut ordered 20 mortar schooners, under the command of Commander David D. Porter, to bombard Forts Jackson and St. Philip beginning on April 18, 1862. Each of the ships' mortars was fired at a rate of once every 10 minutes. During most of a week of heavy shelling, the Union boats lobbed more than 16,000 shells against the Rebel forts. At one point, Fort Jackson caught on fire. Still, the forts did not fall. Farragut, however, was intent on sending his ships up the river. The chain across the channel had been damaged by Union action on April 20, but the Confederates were still in a strong position to repel a Union attack on the water. On the night of April 24, at two A.M., the Union fleet steamed toward New Orleans. Bonfires illuminated the night sky to warn the Confederates.

For more than an hour, the Union and Rebel ships battled one another. The forts fired directly at the invading vessels as Union ships rammed their Confederate counterparts. Fort St. Philip was heavily shelled. The Rebels sent fire ships toward the Union ships and one, the *Hartford,* caught fire. In a hard-fought battle, Farragut's navy, despite taking heavy fire, cut past the forts, having only sustained 210 casualties. Yet the battle for New Orleans had only begun.

Farragut's flotilla had performed remarkably well against the enemy as it advanced on Forts Jackson and St. Philip. The Federals managed to sink many Confederate ships and leave the forts cut off from their river base of support. The Confederates surrendered soon afterward. The Union naval commander took time to order the dead buried and quick repairs made on his ships. Once he and his men had taken care of both their wounded men and vessels, Farragut ordered an advance on a newly vulnerable New Orleans.

In the city, the residents were in a state of panic. The first of the Union vessels reached the city on April 25. The Rebel commander was General Mansfield Lovell, a Maryland West Pointer who had served as New York City's deputy street commissioner before the war. He knew his 3,000 ill-trained, green volunteers, most of whom carried shotguns, would be no match for the cannons of the approaching Union fleet, and he withdrew them from the city, leaving the port town defenseless.

Those who could got out. New Orleans's citizens withdrew $4 million from the city's banks and evacuated. On the docks, Confederates set fire to anything of value, including 15,000 bales of precious southern cotton. Other commodities, including rice, molasses, and sugar, were dumped in the wharf waters. Several boats and naval ships under construction were first set on fire and then allowed to drift toward the approaching enemy.

When Farragut's subordinates tried to bring in their boarding boats to the wharf, they were met with contempt from townspeople. Women spat on them as men vowed to never surrender their city to the Yankees. The occupation took place anyway. The wealthy city was lost to the Rebel cause, and control of the mouth of the Mississippi was crucial to additional Yankee inroads against the enemy between Memphis and New Orleans. In future months, Farragut began advancing farther up the river, and Commander Davis moved south.

Farragut's movements upriver resulted in the fall of the Louisiana city of Baton Rouge and the Mississippi River community of Natchez. These movements left one major Confederate stronghold on the southern portion of the Mississippi River: Vicksburg, Mississippi. Known as the "Gibraltar of the West," Vicksburg enjoyed a marvelous defensive position, facing the Mississippi River and sitting atop a chain of 200-foot bluffs and cliffs that stretched for miles above the river. The Confederates understood the strategic location of the city from the opening days of the war and fortified the river region with 40 heavy guns that menaced all enemy river traffic. In addition, a series of smaller forts were placed along the bluffs and included additional cannon placements and rifle pits. These artillery positions made any approach on Vicksburg from the north a difficult proposal. Marching an army overland was equally daunting for any Union commander. North of the Mississippi River city, nature stood in the way of a federal march: It included 8,000 square miles of "swamp, bayou, and inundated forest. This huge, desolate area, the lowland between the Mississippi and Yazoo Rivers, was impenetrable by troops in any number and could not sustain heavy equipment." [28] Despite these formidable obstacles, it was at Vicksburg that General Grant would eventually lay siege in the spring of 1863.

Throughout the first six months of 1863, Grant's sole objective in the western theater of the Civil War was to capture Vicksburg. As early as the autumn of 1862, Grant intended to march troops directly south from Memphis to Vicksburg, but Confederate opposition was strong. Grant's army had become bogged down, unable to advance. Grant then tried a succession of strategies for approaching Vicksburg.

The Union commander knew that if he sent any military rivercraft down the Mississippi past Vicksburg, they would probably be blown out of the water. Just north of Vicksburg, the river made a hairpin turn. This required a boat to slow down to make the curves in the river just before reaching the Vicksburg bluffs overlooking the river rather than gaining speed and steam in hopes of running the gauntlet of Confederate guns. Grant ordered the digging of a canal to bypass the hairpin turn in the river, as well as Vicksburg itself. However, the digging failed to divert enough water from the Mississippi to float large steamboats and heavy ironclad steamboats in its current. (Remnants of the canal can still be seen in this region of the Mississippi.) Grant's men tried to divert water from Lake Providence, located 50 miles north of Vicksburg, and deepen other river channels that Grant's boats could use to reach the southern river by bypassing the Mississippi altogether. This, too, failed. Union engineers tried to divert levee water into the Yazoo River north of Vicksburg and float its deepened channel. This also did not succeed. As Union gunboats maneuvered their way through the twisted channels, Confederate axmen cut down trees to block their paths and then felled others to block the gunboats' way out.

After months of failure, Grant finally ordered a fleet of Union vessels to try and run the Vicksburg defensive batteries. On a night in April, Rear Admiral David Porter tried to lead his fleet past the Vicksburg guns under cover of darkness. In his book *Ordeal By Fire*, historian James McPherson describes the difficulties the Union vessels encountered:

> On the moonless night of April 16–17, eleven of Porter's boats drifted quietly downriver toward Vicksburg. Suddenly the sky was lit by bonfires set along the banks by Rebel spotters. The heavy guns of Vicksburg opened on the fleet as the boats churned at full speed past the four-mile gauntlet of shot and shell. Every boat was hit; most were set afire; one sank. But the others got through with only thirteen men wounded. A few nights later, six transports and twelve barges tried the same feat with less luck—six of the barges and one transport . . . went to the bottom, but all crewmen were rescued.[29]

With the success of this gutsy military move, Grant was able to get enough men south of Vicksburg to establish a base 35 miles downriver, and, one week later, began ferrying 30,000 Union troops from Hard Times Plantation on the Louisiana side of the river to Bruinsburg, Mississippi. In his words, Grant described how he felt after the previous six months:

> . . . a degree of relief scarcely ever equaled since . . . I was now in the enemy's country, with a vast river and the stronghold of Vicksburg between me and my base of supplies. But I was on dry ground on the same side of the river with the enemy. All the campaigns, labors, hardships, and exposures, from the month of December previous to this time . . . were for the accomplishment of this one object.[30]

THE TRAGEDY OF THE *SULTANA*

Just two weeks after the end of the Civil War, the Union experienced one of the worst disasters in U.S. naval history. On April 27, while making an upriver trip just a few miles from Memphis, the side-wheel steamboat *Sultana* exploded and sank quickly in the muddy waters of the Mississippi, with a loss of life of 1,700 passengers. These facts alone do not tell the true story of the tragedy of the *Sultana*.

The Sultana was built in 1863 as a model of the latest steamboat design. Launched in Cincinnati, it had been built for long-term service on the western rivers. Many steamers were worn out after less than a decade of constant river use, but the *Sultana's* designers planned for their boat to last for many decades. The problem of shipboard explosions—which usually took place when the engine pressure became too high, causing a rupture in the boiler—had been solved with the introduction of special safety features, including gauges that automatically opened when the internal boiler pressure reached 150 psi (pounds per square inch). The *Sultana* was also equipped with three fire hoses and pumps, 30 fire buckets, five fire axes, and life jackets, a rarity on boats of that day. The *Sultana* was not to fall prey to the usual disasters that often killed steamboats within five years of their launch.

As the war ended in April 1865, the federal army enlisted steamboat captains to provide passage for Union troops who had been held in Confederate prison camps, paying $5 per passenger. By just delivering one load of Civil War POWs, a boat captain could make a quick and large profit. The *Sultana* was one of several steamboats that docked at Vicksburg to pick up such passengers. As the *Sultana* prepared to take on Union passengers, one of its boilers developed a serious leak. Rather than take several days to have the repair done right, Captain J. Cass Mason ordered a quick patch job. To wait for such a repair would mean that the *Sultana* might lose out on the quick money to be made in taking war veterans back to the north.

Despite his better judgment and perhaps blinded by greed, the captain accepted passengers on his damaged boat. Union officers placed 2,300 POWs one-by-one onboard the *Sultana,* a number far too large for the boat to carry.

Just two weeks later, on May 14, General Ulysses S. Grant captured Jackson, Mississippi, causing the withdrawal of a Confederate army under the command of Joseph E. Johnston. This victory opened the way for Grant to move on one of the final

(The *Sultana* was registered to carry only 376 passengers!) Captain Mason assured the officers that his boat had carried that same number of passengers on other trips upriver. The soldiers were

> packed in so tightly they could barely stand. The POWs pushed and squeezed themselves onto the top or hurricane deck, the middle or second deck, and the main deck. After their experiences in the Southern prison camps, they could take anything to get back to the North and home to their families as quickly as possible.[*]

For a little more than two days (April 24–26), the *Sultana* paddled upriver, until it finally docked at Memphis to take on coal. That night, after embarking again upriver, the patched boiler blew apart, sending debris throughout the boat and setting the *Sultana* ablaze. Chaos took over. The smokestacks fell down on the boat, killing several soldiers and crushing the hurricane deck. In a panic, many of the startled and frightened men jumped overboard. Most could not swim, and the river was moving swiftly, drowning hundreds. In the darkness, the fires of the *Sultana* lit the night sky, revealing the scope of the tragedy. Hundreds of lifeless bodies floated in the waters around the doomed riverboat.

In the aftermath of the explosion and fire, 1,700 passengers, most of them POWs, were killed. Only 800 onboard the *Sultana* survived the immediate tragedy, but 200 of them later died of their wounds and injuries. The number of casualties of the *Sultana* disaster would prove greater by nearly 200 than the number lost on the ocean liner *Titanic* when it sank at sea more than half a century later.

The remains of the steamboat slipped downriver and finally sank near Memphis, the boat's last major stop on a trip doomed to destruction. Thousands of Union soldiers had managed to survive the harsh conditions of Confederate prison camps, but they did not survive the deadly combination of greed, poor judgment, and faulty equipment.

[*] Quoted in Ambrose and Brinkley, *The Mississippi*, 148.

Confederate blocks to Union traffic on the Mississippi River: Vicksburg, Mississippi.

By late May 1863, Grant began a siege of Vicksburg that lasted for six weeks. Inside, the city's civilian population experienced

The Union capture of the Mississippi River was a culmination of individual naval victories, like the one shown in this print from 1862. Union leaders moved up the Mississippi from New Orleans, capturing specific ports. In 1863, General Ulysses S. Grant began a siege of one of the last Confederate strongholds at Vicksburg, Mississippi. After six weeks of attacks the city fell, opening the river to Union control.

the horrors of mortar bombardments and a dwindling food supply. They dug caves and tunnels into hillsides to serve as bomb shelters. In the final days of the siege, the trapped southerners—soldiers and civilians alike—were forced to eat mule meat, their pet animals, and even rats. The only army in the field close enough to possibly relieve those trapped in Vicksburg, Joe Johnston's force of 30,000, was simply too small to face Grant's combined force of 70,000 men.

On July 3, many of General John C. Pemberton's soldiers sent him a petition stating, "If you can't feed us, you had better surrender." Pemberton did just that on July 4. With Pemberton's surrender, Grant received 31,000 prisoners, 172 artillery pieces, 60,000 rifles and muskets, and a huge quantity of ammunition. As word spread downriver, another Confederate holdout, Port Hudson, surrendered to Union forces on July 8. Few military victories during the Civil War had a greater effect on the Union and the ultimate outcome of the divisive conflict. The fall of Vicksburg was a major strategic win that opened the Mississippi River to uninterrupted Union traffic. For the first time during the Civil War, the Mississippi River was solidly in Union hands. In the words of President Lincoln, "The Father of Waters again goes unvexed to the sea."[31]

6

Taming the
Father of Waters

With the coming of the Civil War and the passing of the golden age of steamboats, the Mississippi River experienced significant changes in the later decades of the nineteenth century and the early twentieth century. The war had brought the steamboat river trade to a grinding halt, and the postwar steamers soon saw a new form of competition: the railroads.

Railways had reached the Mississippi even before the war began. The first railroad bridge across the Mississippi River opened for business in 1856. The bridge spanned the river between the Illinois town of Rock Island and Davenport, Iowa. Others soon followed. More businesses began shipping goods and freight on the new and ever-expanding railroads, with their cheaper rates and extensive reach across the country. Before the Civil War, railroad construction had been limited to the states east of the Mississippi: 35,000 miles of track had been laid, connecting the regions of the north, south, and Midwest. After the war, railroad construction increased. Between 1865 and 1880, an additional 60,000 miles of track were constructed, with 70,000 more miles built between 1880 and 1890. With each passing decade, shipping and traveling by rail became faster, cheaper, safer, and more dependable.

These new realities in transportation spelled an end to the steamboat era of the nineteenth century. Additional railroads reached the Upper Mississippi throughout the 1870s and 1880s, until, by 1886, the river was spanned by 15 railroad bridges. Low water levels several years in a row during the 1890s helped restrict the flow of river traffic even more. The decline of steamboats and the increase in railroad traffic is easily seen in the example of St. Louis. In 1890, this Mississippi River city was handling 12 times as much rail traffic as it was river transportation. Ten years later, the ratio of rail to river traffic was 32 to 1. By 1906, the gap had widened to more than 100 to 1. The steamboat traffic that survived into the twentieth century was based largely on short and medium runs on the river, and the scope of railroad traffic continued to advance across the nation from coast to coast.

(Continued on page 72)

RAILROADS VERSUS STEAMBOATS

Steamboats provided the first regular traffic of commerce and passengers on the Mississippi River during the nineteenth century, but they eventually had to share the river with another steam-powered form of American transportation: railroads. As Americans moved farther west across the Great Plains and to the Pacific Coast, railroads followed. By the 1850s, the early railroads had reached the eastern banks of the Mississippi and plans were being made to build bridges across the river.

The first bridge constructed for railroad use was built on the Mississippi between Rock Island, Illinois and Davenport, Iowa. Opened in the spring of 1856, the rail bridge was greeted with great fanfare. A huge celebration was held at the bridge the day it opened for train traffic as bands played, politicians spoke, and a parade marched in honor of the engineering achievement.

However, just two weeks after the bridge opened, a side-wheeler steamboat, the *Effie Afton*, arrived at the bridge, took on passengers and freight at Davenport, and got back under way upriver. When the steamer reached the bridge, the span opened up to allow passage of the *Effie Afton* through its spans. As the steamboat passed and reached the Rock Island Rapids, however, a paddle wheel shaft tore off, sending the helpless, floating steamer back downriver, where it crashed into the new railroad bridge. In the collision, the cook stove in the boat's galley slipped over and the boat caught on fire. The bridge caught on fire as well. Three hundred head of oxen on the *Effie Afton's* deck leaped into the river to save themselves, along with passengers and crew. Although the hapless boat sank, no one onboard was killed. It took a week to round up all the oxen.

In the wake of the first accident between a Mississippi steamboat and a railroad bridge, the captain of the *Effie Afton* sued the railroad for damages. In his suit, he also called for a ban on the construction of any additional bridges over the Mississippi, calling them a navigation hazard. When a decision on the suit was handed down, the railroad won the case, ensuring the construction of future bridges across the great waterway.

Ten years later, the U.S. Coast Guard did declare the Rock Island Railroad

Many in the steamboat industry were not happy with the growing popularity of railroads in the mid-nineteenth century, fearing a loss of income and calling the bridges navigation hazards, after accidents like the collision between the steamer *Effie Afton* and the Rock Island Railroad Bridge. However, by the turn of the twentieth century, steamboats were nearly obsolete, as evidenced by the proliferation of rail yards, like the one in this photograph from St. Louis in 1900.

Bridge a hazard to navigation, and the bridge steamboat pilots had come to refer to as the "Gate of Death" was torn down and replaced with another rail bridge of a safer design.

The 1856 suit was a victory for the lawyer hired by the railroad to present their case, an attorney from Springfield, Illinois: Abraham Lincoln.

(Continued from page 69)

During the latter decades of the nineteenth century, much of the Mississippi River traffic was no longer centered on steamboats but on towboat operations and barge companies.

The Mississippi Valley Transportation Company of St. Louis, popularly known as "the Barge Line," opened for business in 1866. The company used towboats to push large barges loaded with cargo up and down the river. Such a delivery system proved profitable and, by 1881, the line was shipping 3 million bushels of agricultural products to market monthly. By 1900, tows were transporting barges loaded with between 30,000 and 50,000 tons of goods. Tows also delivered great rafts of trees felled in north central logging camps. These log deliveries might measure as large as 1,000 feet in length. With the capacity of shipping such large quantities of goods and raw materials along the river by using tows and barges, river traffic was able to compete with the ever-expanding railroads of the day. Shipping in such bulk quantities was cheaper by water than by rail. Although barge traffic was hampered by low water levels between 1890 and 1910, the federal government initiated a program to dredge a Mississippi River channel of at least nine feet, and, during the early decades of the twentieth century, 26 locks and dams were built on the river between St. Louis and St. Paul to help encourage river traffic.

Even as the Mississippi was experiencing changes from steamboats to barges, various groups, including the Army Corps of Engineers, continued making attempts to change the river's course, to alter and even out its excesses and harness the great power of the river. Some of these efforts to tame the great Father of Waters were successful, but others proved in time to be miserable failures.

Many of the man-made alterations to the Mississippi River have come at the hands of the United States Army Corps of Engineers. First established in 1802 and trained at the U.S. Military Academy at West Point, the Corps of Engineers has carried out multiple water control projects on many of America's rivers since its formation. No river has experienced

The golden age of steamboats hit its peak in the mid-nineteenth century but declined rapidly after the Civil War. As railroads spread from coast to coast, they took over for steamboats as a faster, cheaper, more dependable way to ship and travel. The first rail bridge across the Mississippi opened in 1856 and today there are 34 rail bridges spanning the river, including this one in Natchez, Mississippi, photographed in 1996.

more change brought about by the Corps than the Mississippi.

The first efforts the Corps of Engineers made to harness the raw power of the river took place in 1822, just before the advent of the steamboat era. A pair of engineers, S. Bernard and Joseph G. Tolten, came to the river and carried out the first official survey of the Mississippi while studying how the river might be altered to improve navigation. In their report, they proposed the construction of locks and other river construction projects. However, decades passed before any real attempts were launched.

In the meantime, the river experienced its greatest flood of the nineteenth century in 1828.

In 1852, the Corps of Engineers set out to make their mark on the river. One engineer, Charles Ellet, completed both a topographic and hydrographic survey of the Mississippi Delta region. His work on the river produced a report in which Ellet and others advocated increased federal responsibility for flood control of the lower Mississippi, as well as a comprehensive plan for preventing trouble by constructing levees, or artificial earthen walls; reservoirs; and diversion channels. Preliminary efforts were put in place to begin implementing Ellet's suggestions, but they were interrupted by the outbreak of the Civil War in 1861. During the war, any local efforts to construct levees and other water control systems deteriorated and fell into disrepair. In 1862, the second year of the war, the Mississippi experienced yet another disastrous flood, which increased the destruction of the river's few levees. Military actions during the war also destroyed earlier efforts to control the river. General Grant, during his 1863 campaign to capture Vicksburg, ordered the destruction of the Yazoo levee in order to bypass the river and deliver troops closer to his Confederate target. When the Civil War finally ended in the spring of 1865, the Mississippi was as wild a river as it had been in centuries.

During the 1870s, Congress once again made control of the Mississippi a major goal and established the Mississippi River Commission. This federal agency was given an extensive mandate and was authorized to

> take into consideration and mature such a plan or plans and estimates as will correct, permanently locate, and deepen the channel and protect the banks of the Mississippi River, improve and give safety and ease of navigation thereof, prevent destructive floods, promote and facilitate commerce, trade, and postal service.[32]

The six-man commission included three Corps of Engineers officers and three civilians, all trained as civil engineers. The commission, however, was slow in approaching the problems of the river, and yet another flood took place, this time in 1882, inundating the Mississippi Delta region and "causing staggering losses in Arkansas and Louisiana as houses were swept away in the torrent."[33]

After the 1882 flood tragedy, the Army Corps of Engineers set out to take control of the violent excesses of the Mississippi. Over a period of several decades, the Corps oversaw the construction of dozens of locks and dams on the upper reaches of the Mississippi, from Minneapolis–St. Paul to St. Louis, a distance of the river measuring nearly 670 miles. Over that length of the river, the Mississippi drops in elevation by 420 feet. The Corps engineers hoped that these efforts would help harness the river.

Much of the resulting work on the river was carried out by the Mississippi River Commission and the Army Corps of Engineers working together. The Corps built levees to hold the river in its course, even when Mississippi water levels were high and prone to flooding. However, the more contained the river became, the more volatility it had. Along the Lower Mississippi, from Cairo, Illinois, to the Gulf of Mexico, the levees reined the river in so tightly that they eliminated all spillways and breaks in the river. A major flood therefore would pose just as significant a problem for those living just beyond the river's levee banks as before. Floods did, in fact, continue, with major events occurring in 1912 and 1913 and smaller flooding in 1884, 1890, 1897, and 1903. Harnessing the river proved more difficult than the experts ever imagined.

Yet the Army Corps of Engineers continued pursuing its difficult mission to make the Mississippi into a controllable river. After the dual floods of 1912 and 1913, Congress passed the 1917 Flood Control Act, providing the Mississippi River Commission with $45 million for flood protection. Levee designs were examined and modified. Sections of the river were dredged to specified depths and dams and flood control projects continued. In 1926, the Army Corps Chief of Engineers wrote in the Corps *Annual Report,* "It may be stated that in a general way the improvement is providing a safe and adequate channel for navigation and is now in condition to prevent the destructive effects of floods." [34] Yet for all the confidence of the Army Corps of Engineers after more than 40 years of effort harnessing the river, the Mississippi would soon prove its power during some of the most severe flooding in the recorded history of the great river.

The year 1927 witnessed the elements of nature in their rawest forms. The Mississippi Valley was inundated with great storms, torrential rains, tornadoes, and even earthquakes. That spring, the skies opened up and delivered long, drenching weeks of endless rain. As one eyewitness along the river stated it, "It started raining, and it just never did stop." [35] For many longtime residents of the river and those who knew its history, the flood that year was like nothing the river had produced within the previous two centuries.

Nature added its extremes to the equation, but the horrific Flood of 1927 was caused by a variety of man-made factors as well. Logging operations along the river's main channel and along tributary arteries had cleared thousands of acres of land, land that had become, in effect, tilled soil, "robbing the water of a place to pause before running down to the Gulf." [36] Rainwater came down in torrential sheets and filled the various feeder streams and tributaries, which in turn emptied into the Mississippi's main channel, bounded on both sides by high earthen dams constructed by the Army Corps of Engineers. A wet winter had caused the Mississippi to remain unseasonably high; as the rains came in the spring, the massive volume of water reached the brims of the dikes, threatening to overflow. Witnesses watched astonished as 20-foot-tall levees filled, bringing boats to the top. There was so much water seeking an escape that it began to back up in the Mississippi's tributaries. For several days, the high level of water in the Ohio River caused the river to flow back upstream.

As cities and towns emerged along the banks of the Mississippi and the river gained importance in the United States economy, the Army Corps of Engineers worked to tame it. The Corps spent decades dredging the river and building levees, locks, and dams, like the one being constructed here in Illinois in 1938, in hopes of preventing floods and keeping the waterway open for travel. These precautions were not foolproof, however, as proven by the mass destruction caused by flooding in 1927.

Even as the whole Mississippi Valley system became water-soaked and unstable, Army Corps of Engineers Major Donald Connolly remained certain that the river's artificial levees would hold against the pressures of the river. On April 9, he gave his public assurances: "We are in condition to hold all the water in sight."[37] However, over the next two weeks, Major Connolly's promises were proven wrong as the levee system was strained to the breaking point. Finally, on April 21, the levees were breached at two places: Pendleton, Arkansas, and Mound Landing, Mississippi. The result was the worst flooding ever seen in the region.

For two months, the Mississippi knew no boundaries. So mighty was the rush of water created when the levees finally broke that eyewitnesses compared it to "a tornado, a strong wind, Niagara Falls, a deep animal growl."[38] Although floodwaters spread out across seven states in the Lower Mississippi region, three states—Mississippi, Arkansas, and Louisiana—were the hardest hit. Along 1,000 miles of the Lower Mississippi River, floodwaters fanned out as far as 100 miles from the river itself. Although the levee on the east bank of the Lower Mississippi only broke at one place—Mound Landing—the resulting floodwaters covered more than 2.3 million acres and displaced nearly 18,000 people. More than 5 million acres of land in Arkansas were flooded. Much of Louisiana was flooded, especially after the break in the levee at Cabin Teele, Louisiana, which resulted in 26,000 square miles being covered with floodwaters. When all accounts were tallied, the major levee system designed to hold the water of the Mississippi experienced 42 major breaks and nearly 80 less-significant levee breaches.

The numbers reveal the extent of the magnitude of this cataclysmic event on the Mississippi. After the waters receded, nearly 17 million acres of land had been flooded. Two hundred thousand homes and other buildings had been destroyed or damaged. The Red Cross provided services and help to more than 330,000 people. Approximately 500 people were killed. Six thousand boats were utilized to rescue those stranded by the flood. The damage caused by the great flood that year reached $1.5 billion.

Historian Pete Daniel describes the scope and aftermath of the Flood of 1927:

> In essence, the Mississippi River had reclaimed its alluvial plain, and only a few levee tops, telephone poles, housetops, Indian mounds, and trees protruded above the flood. Whether one blames poor engineering, overcutting by loggers, improper contour plowing by farmers, or simply attributes it to an act of God, the Mississippi flood of 1927 marks the ultimate high water. It is a record the population of the area is anxious to see stand forever.[39]

7

The Modern
Mississippi

After the extraordinary flooding in 1927, Congress once again recommitted itself to flood control on the Mississippi. In 1928, another Flood Control Act was passed, earmarking new spending on controlling the Mississippi. The new law created yet another agency, the Mississippi River and Tributaries (MR&T) Project. The purpose of this new federal program was to develop a complete and systematic system of flood control for the entire region.

Within 10 years of the Flood of 1927, the Corps of Engineers had dredged out 64 million cubic yards of earth in an effort to raise the heights of 600 miles of levees banking the Lower Mississippi. In addition, throughout the 1930s and 1940s, the agency established river cutoffs, which resulted in shortening the lower reaches of the river by 150 miles. These efforts increased the river's ability to handle floodwaters and reduced flood heights. In Arkansas City, Arkansas, for example, the normal river stages dropped by 12 feet, and, at Vicksburg, the river stages were reduced by an average of 6 feet. The government also monitored the building of new levees, many of them secondary, erected as much as five miles away from the river to handle spillover if the actual riverbank levees ever failed in the future. Other water projects were constructed on tributaries as flood control efforts.

Trade and commerce on the river continued to be an important part of life on the Mississippi. By the 1930s, the modern towboat came into use on the Mississippi. These models featured diesel engines and screw propellers, abandoning the long-standing use of the sternwheel. It was the new diesel-powered tows that helped deliver "30 billion ton-miles of oil, sulfur, coal, steel, wheat, and many other bulk commodities"[40] along the Mississippi and other inland river systems during World War II. The diesel tows have continued to provide a valuable economic service on the Mississippi River.

Major flood control projects soon became part of President Franklin Roosevelt's New Deal programs, designed to provide jobs during the Great Depression and solve national and regional problems at the same time. In Montana, for example, the federal government began construction on the Fort Peck Dam in 1933 to control flooding on the Missouri River. When completed in 1940, this dam became the largest earth-filled dam in the United States. The dam resulted in the formation of a man-made reservoir, Fort Peck Lake, which covers an area measuring 150 miles by 6 miles. Other dams were built on the Missouri throughout the 1940s, 1950s, and 1960s. It was hoped that such projects would eliminate flooding on the Mississippi.

Yet floods on the river have continued to plague the inhabitants of the Mississippi River system throughout the twentieth century. After the 1927 inundation, Mississippi endured floods in 1929, 1937, 1945, 1950, 1973, 1975, 1979, 1983, 1993, and 2001. Many of those flood years produced minor flooding events, but the 1993 flooding was the worst since 1927. Heavy rain and snowfall throughout the winter of 1992–93 resulted in a region water-logged before the spring rains even arrived. When those rains did begin to fall, they were relentless. Across some portions of the Midwest, rain fell for 49 days in a row. The tributary rivers filled to capacity, and the Mississippi flooded its banks. In a herculean effort to control the overflow of the Mississippi and its tributaries, thousands of people volunteered to fight the flood by placing hundreds of thousands of sandbags along the riverbanks. Most of these efforts proved inadequate.

Unlike the 1927 flooding, which was centered in the Lower Mississippi region, the 1993 floods covered the Upper Mississippi states. As a result, floodwaters covered portions of nine states: the Dakotas, Nebraska, Kansas, Missouri, Iowa, Wisconsin, Minnesota, and Illinois. Towns were swamped with floodwater, and thousands of people were forced to evacuate their homes and businesses. The 1993 flooding was not as severe in the Midwest as the 1927 flood had been in the Lower Mississippi Valley, but the 1993 disaster led many Americans to call on the federal government once again to do something. Historian

Despite all the work of the Army Corps of Engineers, the Mississippi and its tributaries still flood every few years. This photograph from 1973 is one example of spring floods along the river in Missouri. The threat of floods does not discourage the 12 million residents living along the river or the businesses that rely on the river for success.

Stephen Ambrose describes the government's new policy following the 1993 flood:

> Instead of building more levees, the federal government
> began a process of buying whole towns or parts of them,

along with farms, on the flood plain and moving the residents to higher ground. Moving people would cost less than rebuilding levees and paying for flood relief. Let the river spread rather than rise and try to hold it in, was the idea. Within two years, 8,000 families had sold their property to the government and moved to higher ground.[41]

Today, flood control on the Mississippi remains a crazy quilt of man-made dams and reservoirs, spillways and locks, levees, channel stabilization, gated drainage structures, pumping stations, and high hopes. Yet, even today, with all the human efforts, resources, money, and expert planning that has gone into flood control measures on the Mississippi over the past two centuries, the words of the great Missouri writer Mark Twain still ring true: "One who knows the Mississippi will promptly aver—not aloud, but to himself—that ten thousand River Commissions . . . cannot tame that lawless stream, cannot curb it or confine it, cannot say to it, Go here, or Go there, and make it obey; cannot save a shore which it has sentenced."[42]

Today, the Mississippi remains an important artery of commerce, trade, entertainment, and tourism. It is also home to millions of people who live in great river cities from St. Paul to St. Louis to New Orleans. In all, the Mississippi Valley is home to 12 million residents who live in 125 counties and parishes that border the great American river. Four million people rely on the Mississippi for their source of drinking water. Riverboats may still be seen on the river, but few work the river as they did in the golden era of steamers during the nineteenth century. Gigantic paddle-wheel replicas of that bygone age, such as the *Delta Queen* and *Mississippi Queen,* still ply the river as part of the tourist trade. Tourism is an important part of the modern legacy of the Mississippi River. Every year, millions of people visit and vacation along the river or in its nearby cities, parks, historical sites, refuges, lakes, and other attractions. They make pilgrimages to the

St. Louis Gateway Arch, a magnificent monument to the American frontier created by President Jefferson's purchase of Louisiana in 1803. This immense, curving, stainless steel giant dominates the St. Louis skyline, reaching 630 feet above the Mississippi River below. (Unfortunately, the designer of the Arch, architect Eero Saarinen, died in 1968, seven years before the structure was completed.)

All along the river, hunting and fishing remain important industries. Throughout the river's flyway, the north–south migratory route followed by various waterfowl, hunting generates $60 million annually, and sport fishing is worth $100 million in income to the region. Many tourists are Americans, but many thousands are foreign tourists, who spend more than $2.5 billion visiting sites in the states bordering the Mississippi River.

A modern-day tour of the Mississippi doesn't even require tourists to get their feet wet. During the 1930s, the federal government established the Mississippi River Parkway Commission (MRPC) to establish a highway system along the Mississippi. Today, that system is known as the Great River Road. The highway follows the Mississippi on both sides from Canada to the Gulf of Mexico and is one of the oldest, longest, and most scenic byways in America. For 3,000 miles, a Mississippi traveler can drive his or her car along 10 Mississippi River states and the Canadian provinces of Ontario and Manitoba. All along the route, scenery, history, and wildlife combine to create a complete river experience. The river is never far away, and the highway markers—green and white, featuring a riverboat pilotwheel—serve as constant reminders. There are 87 federal parks and refuge areas along the Great River Road, as well as 1,100 National Historic Register sites. The road is sometimes flanked by plantation houses, architectural reminders of an era that died with the Civil War. More than 150 visitor centers, interpretative centers, and museums dot the river highway, explaining not only the river's past but also its present and its future.

The river continues to serve as home to great barge tows. Many of these flat, box-shaped vessels stretch in length to 170 feet and to 45 feet in width and are powered by diesel engines boasting 5,000 horsepower. Such great movers of produce along America's greatest waterway deliver 20 percent of the nation's coal, one-third of its petroleum, and 50 percent of its exported grains from one port to another. Each year, the Mississippi River provides a delivery route for nearly 500 million tons of cargo. Along the lazy, wider stretches of the Lower Mississippi, towboats push as many as 30 barges in one trip. That many barges are often loaded with as much as 45,000 tons of cargo among them. To carry that much on land would require nearly 500 railroad boxcars or 2,000 tractor trailer loads! Much of this river freight reaches docks in the Delta, in New Orleans, where it is transferred to great ocean-going ships and carried to markets around the world. To ensure that these ships can safely enter the mouth of the Mississippi, the Army Corps of Engineers maintains an entrance channel depth of 45 feet.

The Corps has always worked to keep the river under control, but others have continued to dominate the river in other ways. Since the days following the Civil War, bridge after bridge has spanned the mighty river, delivering trains and automobiles on their way across America. By the mid-1990s, the Mississippi River had been spanned by 169 bridges. The majority of these cross-river systems—122 in all—were highway bridges. The remainder were 34 railroad bridges, a dozen dual-purpose highway–railroad bridges, and one pipeline bridge. One of the earliest—Eads Bridge—still spans the waterfront at St. Louis and stretches across the river to Illinois. This impressive, well-designed bridge has proven the test of time. Erected in 1874 as the first steel-truss structure in America, Eads Bridge helped turn St. Louis from an important steamboat river town to a railroad hub in the Midwest.

As the Mississippi River continues to flow into the twenty-first century, it represents one of the most completely engineered

For more than a century, the U.S. government has adjusted and manipulated the Mississippi River and its banks to make it a safer, more profitable transportation route and a more appealing place to live. Even today, workers continue to build systems to alter the river's flow and prevent flooding, like this structure on the river in Louisiana.

and manipulated natural features in the United States. The river's floodplain has been artificially altered and twisted to make room for vast agricultural programs and more river communities, including small towns and large metropolitan centers. Since the 1940s, approximately 80 percent of the river's wetlands have been drained. The river has been channeled artificially many times over by levees and floodwalls, and new structures intended to force the river into yet another course of flow continue to be built.

In addition to the constant and looming questions concerning the potential for future floods along the Mississippi River and its tributaries, environmental quality issues continue to plague the future of the great American river. Questionable use of the river has led to serious concerns about the levels of toxic chemicals, wastewater, and other kinds of pollution from manufacturing, extensive farming operations, and other causes. The river is all too frequently a dumping reservoir for petrochemical and crude oil discharges. Chemicals used in farming, including fertilizers, herbicides, pesticides, and animal waste runoff from stockyards and hog operations, add to the lowering of water quality along the river. Every year, hundreds of tons of such wastes and chemicals drain off of millions of acres of American farms. Some experts blame fertilizer runoff for the increase in algae growth in the Mississippi, the Delta, and the Gulf of Mexico, where the river's waters eventually drain. Studies have indicated that chemicals found in drinking water from the Mississippi may be linked to increases in cancer rates. The same studies have linked increases in lung cancer rates to those living in close proximity to petrochemical plants along the Mississippi.

Some significant steps have been taken to help solve these and other environmental issues. Environmental laws—such as the Safe Drinking Water Act, the Clean Air Act, and the Clean Water Act—provide a national framework for designing a large-scale plan for improving water conditions along the Mississippi River. These acts, plus a large package of federal executive orders, state and local laws, and extensive environmental education programs, are responsible for helping make more people aware of the importance of protecting the nation's waterways, including the Mississippi River Valley.

The Mississippi has always served as a vital link in the economies of Americans from the first Indians who lived along its banks to millions of people who live not only close to the river but also inside its massive river valley system. Balancing environmental issues and the economic benefits provided by the river has often proven tricky at best and seemingly impossible otherwise. However, as more and more Americans become aware of the dangers of regularly damaging the environment, they may be prepared to accept limits on the future use of the Mississippi River. For all Americans, the Mississippi River should be viewed as an important part of our national and natural heritage. This great symbol of America's diverse history, development, and expansion must remain a source of pride, a historical treasure, a resource to cherish, and a complicated ecosystem to protect and preserve.

CHRONOLOGY AND TIMELINE

10,000 B.C. The Mississippi River is created during the final stages of the most recent ice age, the Wisconsin Glaciation.

A.D. 700–1500 The people of the final era of Mound Builders, the Mississippian Culture, build their homes along the banks of the Mississippi, including the village of Cahokia.

1519 Spanish explorer Alonzo Alvarez de Pineda arrives at the mouth of the Mississippi.

1541 Spanish explorer Hernando DeSoto reaches the banks of the Mississippi after exploring the south-eastern portion of the modern-day United States.

1673 French explorers Father Jacques Marquette and Louis Joliet reach the Mississippi River from the north and canoe as far south as the Arkansas River on the Lower Mississippi.

1541
DeSoto reaches the banks of the Mississippi.

1840–60
The golden era of steamboating on the river.

10,000 B.C.
Mississippi River created at the end of the most recent ice age.

1812
The first steamboat reaches New Orleans by way of the Ohio and Mississippi rivers

1803
The Louisiana Purchase is completed.

10,000 B.C.　**A.D. 1700**　**1800**　**1890**

A.D. 700–1500
Era of the Mound Builders

1718
New Orleans is settled by the French.

1856
The first railroad bridge is opened for business across the river.

1673
Father Jacques Marquette and Louis Joliet reach the Mississippi River from the north.

1764
St. Louis is established by the French.

1861–65
The American Civil War interrupts normal commercial traffic.

1682 French explorer and entrepreneur René-Robert Cavelier, Sieur de La Salle explores much of the Mississippi, floating the river from the north to its mouth in the Gulf of Mexico.

1718 The French establish the settlement of New Orleans on the Lower Mississippi.

1764 The French establish the town of St. Louis on the Mississippi.

1784–1788 The Spanish close off the Mississippi River to American river traffic.

1795 Thomas Pinckney signs treaty with Spain, reopening the river and New Orleans to the Americans.

1803 President Thomas Jefferson's diplomats in Paris purchase the Louisiana Territory, making the Mississippi an American river.

1900–20s
The U.S. Army Corps of Engineers constructs 26 locks and dams on the upper Mississippi.

1993
Severe flooding again occurs along the upper reaches of the river.

1917
Terrible floods in 1912 and 1913 impel the passage of the Flood Control Act

1900   *1950*   *2000*

1930s
Modern rowboats come into use. The U.S. government creates the Parkway Planning Commission to establish the Great River Road.

1927
The Flood of 1927 causes perhaps the worst flooding in the river's history.

1805   American explorers Lewis and Clark camp with their men on the Illinois side of the Mississippi. Later that year, Zebulon Pike, another American explorer, sets out upriver to find the source of the Mississippi, which he identifies incorrectly.

1812   The first steamboat reaches New Orleans after traveling down the Ohio and Mississippi Rivers.

1823   The first steamboat travels north from St. Louis and reaches St. Paul, Minnesota.

1832   Henry P. Schoolcraft, Indian agent and mineralogist, reaches the source of the Mississippi and names it Lake Itasca. That same year, the first large-scale steamboat service on the river was established (Ohio and Mississippi Mail Line).

1840–60   The Mississippi River experiences its golden era of steamboating.

1849   A dramatic steamboat disaster occurs in St. Louis when fire breaks out along the wharf, ultimately destroying 23 steamboats.

1850   Nearly $100 million worth of goods is being shipped through New Orleans annually.

1852   Congress passes the Steamboat Act, requiring steamboat companies and owners to "correct the unsatisfactory conditions on river paddle-wheel steamboats."

1856   The first railroad bridge across the Mississippi River is opened for business.

1861–1865   The American Civil War interrupts regular commercial traffic on the Mississippi, signaling the decline of the great steamboat era on the river.

1862 The Confederate city of New Orleans falls to Union naval forces.

1863 Grant captures the Mississippi River stronghold of Vicksburg.

1865 The steamboat *Sultana* explodes, killing 1,700 passengers, most of whom were newly freed Union prisoners-of-war. The *Sultana*'s destruction marks the greatest loss of life in the river's history.

1874 Eads Bridge, built at St. Louis, is completed. It is the first steel-truss structure in America.

1882 The Mississippi River Valley experiences one of its most severe floods of modern times.

1890 With the advent of the railroad, rail commerce outdistances Mississippi River traffic in St. Louis 12 times over.

1900 As the steamboat era nearly draws to a close, Mississippi River towboats are becoming the more common form of commercial traffic on the river.

1900–20s The U.S. Army Corps of Engineers constructs 26 locks and dams on the Upper Mississippi, between St. Louis and St. Paul, to help control the river.

1917 After a pair of terrible floods in 1912 and 1913, Congress passes the Flood Control Act, providing the Mississippi River Commission with $45 million for flood protection.

1927 Causing perhaps the worse flooding ever on the Mississippi, the Flood of 1927 covers more than 17 million acres, destroyed 200,000 homes and buildings, and displaced thousands of river residents.

1928   Congress passes another Flood Control Act, creating the Mississippi River and Tributaries Project, mandated to develop a complete and systematic system of flood control for the Mississippi.

1930s   The modern towboat, with its diesel engines and screw propellers, comes into use on the Mississippi. At the same time, the federal government establishes the Mississippi River Parkway Commission to establish a highway system, known today as the Great River Road, along the Mississippi

1968   The St. Louis Gateway Arch is completed, commanding the cityscape and becoming one of the most recognizable man-made landmarks on the Mississippi.

1993   Severe flooding occurs in the region of the Upper Mississippi.

CHAPTER 1:
The River's First Inhabitants

1. Quoted in Tom Weil, *The Mississippi River: Nature, Culture and Travel Sites Along the "Mighty Mississip"* (New York: Hippocrene Books, Inc.), 13.
2. Quoted in Stephen Ambrose and Douglas Brinkley, *The Mississippi and the Making of a Nation* (Washington, DC: National Geographic Society, 2002), 7.
3. Quoted in Norbury L. Wayman, *Life on the River* (New York: Bonanza Books, 1971), 1–2.
4. Quoted in Tim McNeese, *Illustrated Myths of Native America: The Northeast, Southeast, Great Lakes, and Great Plains* (London: Cassell Books, 1998), 49.
5. Quoted in Bern Keating, *The Mighty Mississippi* (Washington, DC: National Geographic Society, 1971), 93.
6. Quoted in Ann McCarthy, *The Mississippi River* (New York: Crescent Books, 1984), 5.

CHAPTER 2:
The First Europeans

7. Quoted in Hodding Carter, *Lower Mississippi* (New York: Farrar & Rinehart, 1942), 15.
8. Ibid., 21–22.
9. Quoted in McCarthy, *The Mississippi River*, 6.
10. Quoted in William Syme, *Marquette and Joliet: Voyagers on the Mississippi* (New York: William Morrow and Company, 1974), 26.
11. Ibid., 42.
12. Ibid.
13. Quoted in Jacques Marquette, *Voyages of Marquette in the Jesuit Relations, 59* (Ann Arbor, MI: University Microfilms, Inc., 1966).
14. Quoted in Joy Hakim, *The First Americans* (New York: Oxford University Press), 136.
15. Quoted in Marquette, *Voyages,* 141.
16. Quoted in Carter, *Lower Mississippi*, 24.

17. Quoted in McCarthy, *The Mississippi River*, 6.
18. Ibid.
19. Quoted in Wayman, *Life on the River*, 12.
20. Ibid., p. 13.

CHAPTER 4:
Days of Steam

21. Quoted in Ambrose and Brinkley, *The Mississippi*, 84–85.
22. Quoted in Wayman, *Life on the River*, 144.
23. Quoted in Captain Ron Larson, *Upper Mississippi River History: Fact—Fiction—Legend* (Winona, MN: Steamboat Press, 1994), 11.
24. Ibid., 12.
25. Quoted in Wayman, *Life on the River*, 181.
26. Ibid., 165.
27. Quoted in Mark Twain, *Pudd'nhead Wilson* (New York: Penguin Putnam, Inc., Signet Classic, 1964), 22.

CHAPTER 5:
A River Vexed by War

28. Quoted in John S. Blay, *The Civil War* (New York: Bonanza Books, 1958), 168.
29. Quoted in James McPherson, *Ordeal By Fire: The Civil War and Reconstruction* (New York: McGraw-Hill, Inc., 1992), 312.
30. Ibid.
31. Quoted in Roy P. Basler, *The Collected Works of Abraham Lincoln, Vol. VI*, 409.

CHAPTER 6:
Taming the Father of Waters

32. Quoted in Ambrose and Brinkley, *The Mississippi*, 223.
33. Ibid.
34. Quoted in *Annual Report of the Chief of Engineers, United States Army*, 1929, "Mississippi River Commission," 1793.

35. Quoted in Pete Daniel, *Deep'n as It Come: The 1927 Mississippi River Flood* (New York: Oxford University Press, 1977), 7.
36. Ibid., 7.
37. Ibid., 9.
38. Ibid.
39. Ibid., 10.

CHAPTER 7:
The Modern Mississippi

40. Quoted in Wayman, *Life on the Mississippi*, 316.
41. Quoted in Ambrose and Brinkley, *The Mississippi*, 226.
42. Quoted in Daniel, 6.

Ambrose, Stephen, and Douglas G. Brinkley. *The Mississippi and the Making of a Nation.* Washington, D.C.: National Geographic Society, 2002.

Barry, John. *Rising Tide: The Great Mississippi Flood of 1927 and How It Changed America.* New York: Simon & Schuster, 1997.

Billington, Ray Allen. *Westward Expansion, A History of the American Frontier.* New York: The Macmillan Company, 1960.

Blay, John S. *The Civil War.* New York: Bonanza Books, 1958.

Burman, Ben Lucien. *Look Down That Winding River: An Informal Profile of the Mississippi.* New York: Taplinger Publishing Company, 1973.

Carter, Hodding. *Lower Mississippi.* New York: Farrar & Rinehart, 1942.

Chapman, Carl H., and Eleanor F. *Indians and Archaeology of Missouri.* Columbia: University of Missouri Press, 1983.

Daniel, Pete. *Deep'n as It Come: The 1927 Mississippi River Flood.* New York: Oxford University Press, 1977.

DeVoto, Bernard. *The Course of Empire.* Boston: Houghton Mifflin Company, 1952.

Fraiser, Jim. *Mississippi River Country Tales: A Celebration of 500 Years of Deep South History.* Gretna, LA: Pelican Publishing Company, 2001.

Hakim, Joy. *The First Americans.* New York: Oxford University Press, 1993.

Hamilton, Raphael N. *Marquette's Explorations: The Narratives Reexamined.* Madison: University of Wisconsin Press, 1970.

Josephy, Alvin M., Jr. *The Indian Heritage of America.* Boston: Houghton Mifflin Company, 1991.

Joutel, Henri. *The Last Voyage Perform'd by de la Sale.* Ann Arbor, MI: University Microfilms, Inc., 1966.

Keating, Bern. *The Mighty Mississippi*. Washington, D.C.: National Geographic Society, 1971.

Larson, Captain Ron. *Upper Mississippi River History: Fact—Fiction—Legend*. Winona, MN: Steamboat Press, 1994.

Lockwood, C.C. *Around the Bend: A Mississippi River Adventure*. Baton Rouge: Louisiana State University Press, 1998.

Lourie, Peter. *Mississippi River: A Journey Down the Father of Waters*. Honesdale, PA: Boyds Mills Press, 2000.

Marquette, Jacques. *Voyages of Marquette in The Jesuit Relations, 59*. Ann Arbor, MI: University Microfilms, Inc., 1966.

McCarthy, Ann. *The Mississippi River*. New York: Crescent Books, 1984.

McNeese, Tim. *Illustrated Myths of Native America: The Northeast, Southeast, Great Lakes, and Great Plains*. London: Cassell Books, 1998.

McPherson, James. *Ordeal By Fire: The Civil War and Reconstruction*. New York: McGraw-Hill, Inc., 1992.

Ogg, Frederic Austin. *The Opening of the Mississippi*. New York: The Macmillan Company, 1904.

Paxson, Frederic L. *History of the American Frontier, 1763–1893*. Boston: Houghton Mifflin Company, 1924.

Raban, Jonathan. *Old Glory, An American Voyage*. New York: Simon and Schuster, 1981.

Schoolcraft, Henry Rowe. *Travels Through the Northwestern Regions of the United States*. Ann Arbor, MI: University Microfilms, Inc., 1966.

Shaffer, James L., and John T. Tigges. *The Mississippi River: Father of Waters*. Chicago: Arcadia Publishing, 2000.

Smart, Miles M. *Ecological Perspectives of the Upper Mississippi River*. Boston: Dr. W. Junk Publishers, 1986

Sprague, Marshall. *So Vast, So Beautiful a Land: Louisiana and the Purchase.* Boston: Little, Brown and Company, 1974.

Syme, William. *Marquette and Joliet: Voyagers on the Mississippi.* New York: William Morrow and Company, 1974.

Turner, Frederick Jackson. *Rise of the New West: 1819–1829.* Gloucester, MA: Peter Smith Publishers, 1961.

Twain, Mark. *Life on the Mississippi.* New York: Airmont Books, 1965.

———. *Pudd'nHead Wilson.* New York: Penguin Putnam, Inc., Signet Classic, 1964.

Wayman, Norbury L. *Life on the River.* New York: Bonanza Books, 1971.

Weil, Tom. *The Mississippi River: Nature, Culture and Travel Sites Along the "Mighty Mississip."* New York: Hippocrene Books, Inc., 1992.

Whitaker, Arthur Preston. *The Spanish–American Frontier: 1783–1795.* Lincoln: University of Nebraska Press, 1969.

Archaeological Institute of America. "Belle Bonanza." *Archaeology,*
27 February 1998.
www.archaeology.org/magazine.php?page=online/news/belle

INDEX

INDEX

page:

4:   Library of Congress, LC-USZ4-2851
11: © Michael S. Lewis/CORBIS
17: © Bettmann/CORBIS
21: © Bettmann/CORBIS
32: © CORBIS
35: © Bettmann/CORBIS
36: © Bettmann/CORBIS
40: © Bettmann/CORBIS
51: Library of Congress, LC-USZC2-3743
57: © CORBIS

66: Library of Congress, LC-USZC4-4250
71: © CORBIS
73: © Danny Lehman/CORBIS
77: US Army Corps of Engineers
     Digital Visual Library
83: Courtesy National Oceanic &
     Atmospheric Administration (NOAA),
     Historic NWS Collection
87: © Philip Gould/CORBIS

Frontis: © MAPS.com/CORBIS
Cover: © Arthur Rothstein/CORBIS

TIM MCNEESE is an Associate Professor of History at York College in Nebraska. Professor McNeese earned an Associate of Arts degree from York College, a Bachelor of Arts degree in history and political science from Harding University, and a Master of Arts degree in history from Southwest Missouri State University. He is currently in his 27th year of teaching.

Professor McNeese's writing career has earned him a citation in the "Something About the Author" reference work. He is the author of more than fifty books and educational materials on everything from Egyptian pyramids to American Indians. He is married to Beverly McNeese, who teaches English at York College.